# CONT[ENTS]

C000205642

## MapStudio

**0860 10 50 50**

**www.mapstudio.co.za**

**Production:** Braam Smit, Martin Endemann, Charleen Mathys, Ryno Swart,Christine Flemington.
**Research:** Judy Graham, Derek Nel, Anthony Davids.
**Graphic Design & Index:** Braam Smit.
Printed and bound by CTP Book Printers , Cape

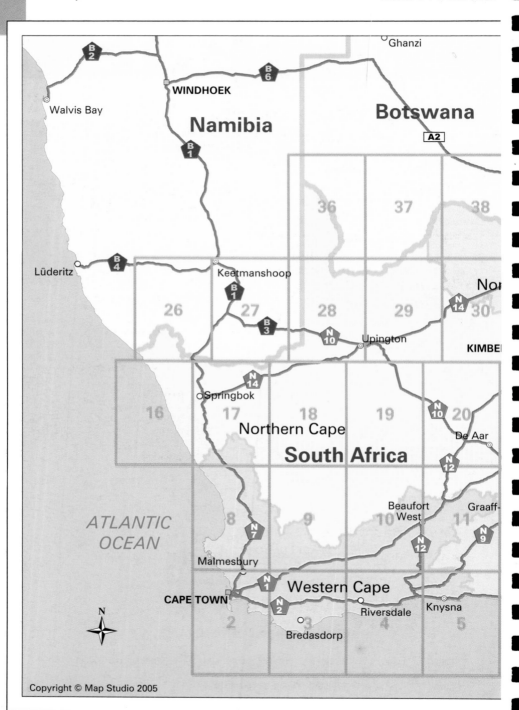

Copyright © Map Studio 2005

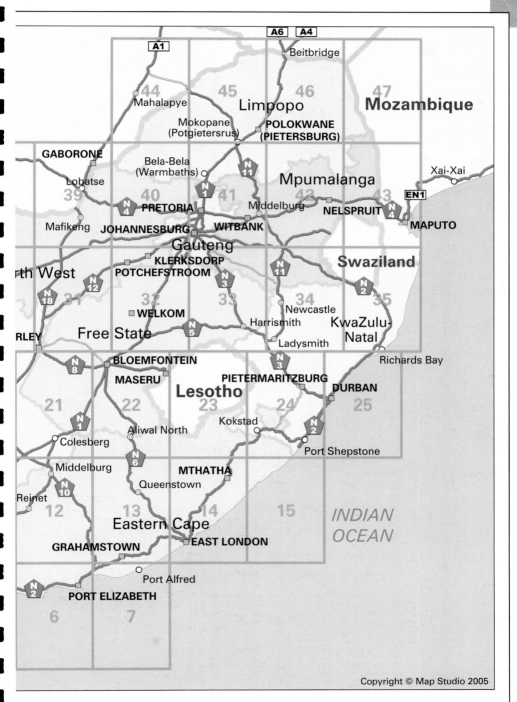

Copyright © Map Studio 2005

# IV Distance Table

| | PRETORIA | PORT ELIZABETH | MTHATHA | MBABANE | MASERU | MAPUTO | MAFIKENG | KIMBERLEY | JOHANNESBURG | GABORONE | EAST LONDON | DURBAN | CAPE TOWN | BLOEMFONTEIN |
|---|---|---|---|---|---|---|---|---|---|---|---|---|---|---|
| BLOEMFONTEIN | 455 | 681 | 570 | 677 | 157 | 862 | 464 | 177 | 398 | 622 | 584 | 634 | 1004 | • |
| CAPE TOWN | 1460 | 769 | 1314 | 1680 | 1160 | 1865 | 1343 | 969 | 1402 | 1501 | 1079 | 1753 | • | 1004 |
| COLESBERG | 682 | 451 | 517 | 903 | 383 | 1085 | 672 | 292 | 624 | 848 | 488 | 860 | 778 | 226 |
| DURBAN | 636 | 984 | 439 | 562 | 590 | 620 | 821 | 811 | 557 | 979 | 674 | • | 1753 | 634 |
| EAST LONDON | 1040 | 310 | 235 | 1238 | 630 | 1301 | 1048 | 780 | 982 | 1206 | • | 674 | 1079 | 584 |
| GABORONE | 350 | 1299 | 1192 | 719 | 702 | 919 | 158 | 538 | 358 | • | 1206 | 979 | 1501 | 622 |
| GEORGE | 1229 | 335 | 880 | 1450 | 913 | 1670 | 1203 | 762 | 1171 | 1361 | 645 | 1319 | 438 | 773 |
| GRAAFF-REINET | 880 | 291 | 503 | 1101 | 599 | 1283 | 854 | 490 | 822 | 1012 | 395 | 942 | 787 | 424 |
| GRAHAMSTOWN | 1057 | 130 | 415 | 1418 | 692 | 1478 | 1065 | 667 | 999 | 1223 | 180 | 854 | 899 | 601 |
| JOHANNESBURG | 58 | 1075 | 869 | 361 | 438 | 555 | 287 | 476 | • | 358 | 982 | 557 | 1402 | 398 |
| KEETMANSHOOP | 1354 | 1429 | 1547 | 1657 | 1283 | 1851 | 1072 | 897 | 1296 | 1230 | 1468 | 1708 | 995 | 1074 |
| KIMBERLEY | 530 | 743 | 747 | 833 | 334 | 1033 | 380 | • | 476 | 538 | 780 | 811 | 962 | 177 |
| LADYSMITH | 414 | 1062 | 517 | 386 | 366 | 529 | 597 | 587 | 356 | 755 | 752 | 248 | 1413 | 410 |
| MAFIKENG | 294 | 1141 | 1034 | 648 | 544 | 848 | • | 380 | 287 | 158 | 1048 | 821 | 1343 | 464 |
| MAPUTO | 545 | 1609 | 1064 | 223 | 815 | • | 848 | 1033 | 555 | 919 | 1301 | 620 | 1865 | 862 |
| MASERU | 488 | 822 | 616 | 633 | • | 815 | 544 | 334 | 438 | 702 | 630 | 590 | 1160 | 157 |
| MBABANE | 372 | 1548 | 1003 | • | 633 | 223 | 648 | 833 | 361 | 719 | 1238 | 562 | 1680 | 677 |
| MTHATHA | 928 | 545 | • | 1003 | 616 | 1064 | 1034 | 747 | 869 | 1192 | 235 | 439 | 1314 | 570 |
| MUSINA | 447 | 1594 | 1392 | 797 | 949 | 687 | 680 | 991 | 505 | 696 | 1501 | 1107 | 1921 | 928 |
| NELSPRUIT | 322 | 1434 | 976 | 173 | 713 | 206 | 635 | 827 | 355 | 672 | 1226 | 707 | 1762 | 757 |
| PIETERMARITZBURG | 557 | 905 | 360 | 640 | 511 | 706 | 742 | 732 | 499 | 900 | 595 | 79 | 1664 | 555 |
| POLOKWANE | 250 | 1383 | 1181 | 504 | 738 | 567 | 569 | 780 | 297 | 485 | 1290 | 886 | 1710 | 706 |
| PORT ELIZABETH | 1133 | • | 545 | 1548 | 822 | 1609 | 1141 | 743 | 1075 | 1299 | 310 | 984 | 769 | 681 |
| PRETORIA | • | 1133 | 928 | 372 | 488 | 545 | 294 | 530 | 58 | 350 | 1040 | 636 | 1460 | 455 |
| UPINGTON | 854 | 933 | 1047 | 1157 | 731 | 1357 | 572 | 397 | 796 | 730 | 968 | 1208 | 894 | 574 |
| WELKOM | 316 | 830 | 718 | 451 | 249 | 775 | 321 | 294 | 258 | 479 | 737 | 564 | 1156 | 153 |

Copyright © Map Studio 2005

Although the greatest care has been taken in compiling the kilometre table and ensuring that the road distances given conform to the latest information available, no responsibility for errors can be accepted by the publishers, who would welcome any suggested amendments. The kilometres indicate the shortest distance between any two places over tarred roads wherever possible.

To find the distance between any two places in the table read down and across the respective connecting columns. An example is given above in which the distance between Cape Town and Port Elizabeth is shown as 769 kilometres.

ATLANTIC OCEAN · INDIAN OCEAN · NAMIBIA · WINDHOEK · BOTSWANA · ZIMBABWE · MOZAMBIQUE · Musina · Polokwane · PRETORIA · Nelspruit · Gaborone · MBABANE · SWAZILAND · Mafikeng · Johannesburg · Welkom · MAPUTO · Kimberley · MASERU · Pietermaritzburg · BLOEMFONTEIN · LESOTHO · Durban · SOUTH AFRICA · Graaff-Reinet · Mthatha · Upington · Grahamstown · East London · CAPE TOWN · George · Port Elizabeth · Keetmanshoop

0   5  10    20    30    40    50km

## Scale 1 : 1 500 000

Tarred          Untarred

Under
Construction

............................................................................ Freeway / National Road

............................................................................ Main Road

............................................................................ Secondary Road

............................................................................ Route Numbers

............................................................................ Toll Route and Toll Plaza

............................................................................ Mountain Pass

15 ........................................................................ Distance in Kilometres

............................................................................ Railway

............................................ International Boundaries / Provincial Boundaries

............................................................................ Water features

............................................................................ Pan

............................................................................ Marsh

............................................................................ National Park and Nature Reserve

............................................................................ Capital or City

............................................................................ Major Town

............................................................................ Secondary Town

............................................................................ Other Town

............................................................................ Settlement

............................................................................ Accommodation

............................................................................ Historical Site

............................................................................ Border Control

............................................................................ Major Airport

............................................................................ Airfield

............................................................................ Major Spot Height

............................................................................ Place of Interest

............................................................................ Waterfall

............................................................................ Battlefeilds

Copyright © Map Studio 2005

54  55  8  56  57

18°00'E  Velddrif  Darling  Moorreesburg  Gouda  Tulbagh  Ceres

Dassen Island  Flower Reserves  R307  Malmesbury  Kasteel  Wolseley
Mission Station  Abbotsdale  Hermon  17
Mamre  22  Soetendal  13
38  Atlantis  R302  Malan  27
Bokpunt  10  10  Kalbaskraal  R45  Bains Kloof
Philadelphia Windmill  **Wellington**
Melkbosstrand  12  7  11  R304  Mbekweni  Du Toitskloof
Bloubergstrand  5  16  R304  **Paarl**  34
Robben Island  12  9  Meilish  HUGUENOT
(World Heritage Site) **Milnerton**  **Durbanville**  TOLL TUNNEL
Table Bay  6  10  16  Wemmershoek
**CAPE TOWN**  **Bellville**  Pniel  Dam
**Parow**  Helshoogte  Groendal
Table Mountain  Kuilsrivier  Kylemore  Fransch-
Llandudno  15  19  **Stellenbosch** Fransch-  hoek
Hout Bay  16  Faure  20  hoek Pass  9
Noordhoek  7  30  Firgrove  Hottentots-Hollands  R321
Kommetjie  20  13  Nat. Res.  Grabouw  Theewaterskloof
Scarborough  Muizenberg  **Somerset**  Houhoek  Dam
Fish Hoek  **Strand**  **West**  22  Pass
**Simon's Town**  Gordons  Sir  Elgin  21  9
Table Mountain  Bay  Lowry's  Botrivier
National Park  13  R44  Pass
Cape of Good Hope  False Bay  Kogelberg  Kleinmond
Cape Point  Nat. Res.  11
Pringle Bay  Hawston  Onrus
SEE PAGES 50 - 51  Betty's  Hermanus
Bay

34°00'S

*A t l a n t i c*

*O c e a n*

SEE PAGES 52 - 53

35°00'S

DA

DB

DC

DD

DE

Copyright © Map Studio 2005

18°00'E  19°00'E

54  55  56  57

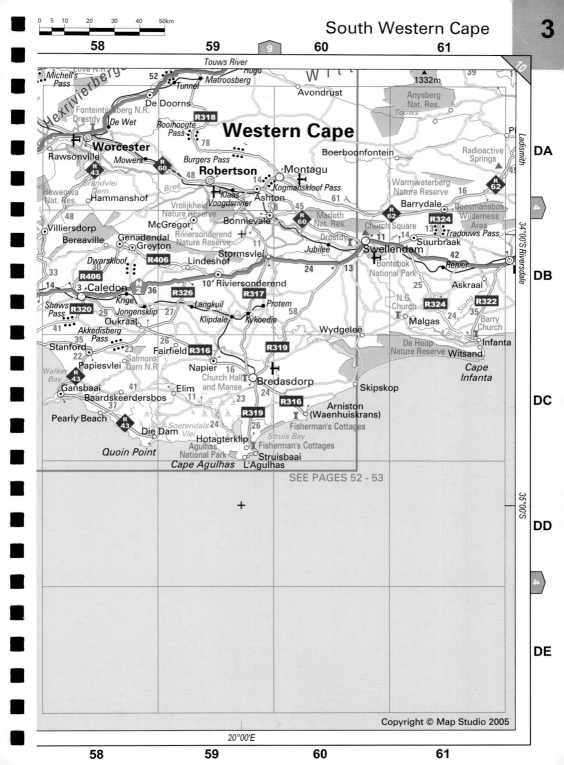

0 5 10 20 30 40 50km

Touws River

Michell's Pass
52
Tunnel
Matroosberg
Hugo
De Doorns
Avondrust
1332m
39
Anysberg Nat. Res.
Touws
Fonteintjiesberg N.R.
Drostdy
De Wet
Rooihoogte Pass
R318
78
**Western Cape**
Boerboonfontein
Radioactive Springs
DA
**Worcester**
Rawsonville
Mowers
R43
R60
Burgers Pass
48
**Robertson**
14
Montagu
Kogmanskloof Pass
61
Warmwaterberg Nature Reserve
16
R62
Brandvlei Dam
Hawequa Nat. Res.
Hammanshof
Bree
Klaas Voogdsrivier
Ashton
8
45
Barrydale
Beosmansbos Wilderness Area
4
48
McGregor
Vrolijkheid Nature Reserve
Bonnievale
Marloth Nat. Res.
R62
R324
13
Tradouws Pass
Villiersdorp
Bereaville
Genadendal
Greyton
Riviersonderend Nature Reserve
Drostdy
Church Square
11
14
Suurbraak
Jubilee
Swellendam
42
DB
Dwarskloof
30
R406
Stormsvlei
Lindeshof
24
13
Bontebok National Park
Renier
25
Askraal
33
R406
10
Riviersonderend
14
3
Caledon
N2
36
R326
Langkuil
R317
Protem
58
N.G. Church
R324
Slang
R322
Shaws Pass
R320
27
Krige
Jongensklip
Klipdale
Kykoedie
Malgas
24
35
Barry Church
Oukraal
Akkedisberg Pass
41
26
Wydgeleë
Bree
Infanta
35
Stanford
23
Salmons Dam N.R.
Fairfield
R316
R319
De Hoop Nature Reserve
Witsand
22
Papiesvlei
Napier
16
Cape Infanta
Walker Bay
R43
Gansbaai
41
Elim
Church Hall and Manse
Bredasdorp
24
Skipskop
DC
Baardskeerdersbos
37
11
23
Pearly Beach
R43
Die Dam
Soetendals Vlei
24
R319
R316
26
Struis Bay
Arniston (Waenhuiskrans)
Fisherman's Cottages
Quoin Point
Hotagterklip
Fisherman's Cottages
Agulhas National Park
Struisbaai
Cape Agulhas
L'Agulhas

SEE PAGES 52 - 53

DD

34°00'S Riversdale

35°00'S

Ladismith
45

DE

20°00'E

Copyright © Map Studio 2005

| | **62** | **63** | **64** | **65** |
|---|---|---|---|---|

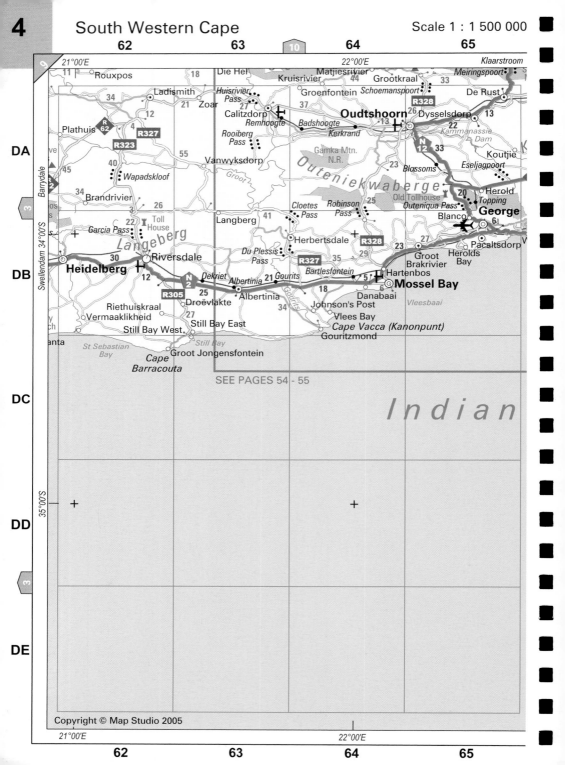

21°00'E

Klaarstroom
Rouxpos
Die Hel
Matjiesrivier
Meiringspoort
Kruisrivier
Grootkraal
33
Ladismith
18
Groenfontein
Schoemanspoort
De Rust
Huisrivier Pass
44
R328
34
21
37
26
22
12
Zoar
27
Calitzdorp
Oudtshoorn
Dysselsdorp
13
Plathuis
R62
4
Remhoogte
Badshoogte
13
Kammanassie Dam
R327
Rooiberg Pass
Kerkrand
N12
33
**DA**
R323
Koutjie
40
55
Vanwyksdorp
Gamka Mtn. N.R.
Eseljagpoort
45
Wapadskloof
23
Blossoms
20
Herold
34
Brandrivier
26
Old Tollhouse
Topping
Outeniqua Pass
**George**
3
Langberg
Cloetes Pass
Robinson Pass
25
Blanco
6
Toll House
Langberg
41
Pacaltsdorp
22
Garcia Pass
27
Herbertsdale
R328
23
Herolds Bay
Langeberg
Du Plessis Pass
35
29
Groot Brakrivier
**DB**
30
Riversdale
Albertinia
21
Gourits
Bartlesfontein
Hartenbos
Dekriet
5
**Heidelberg**
12
N2
Albertinia
18
Danabaai
**Mossel Bay**
R305
25
Droëvlakte
34
Johnson's Post
6
Vleesbaai
Riethuiskraal
27
Vlees Bay
Vermaaklikheid
Still Bay East
Cape Vacca (Kanonpunt)
Still Bay West
Gouritzmond
St Sebastian Bay
Still Bay
Groot Jongensfontein
Cape Barracouta

SEE PAGES 54 - 55

*Indian*

35°00'S

Copyright © Map Studio 2005

21°00'E        22°00'E

| | **62** | **63** | **64** | **65** |
|---|---|---|---|---|

0 5 10 20 30 40 50km

66 67 **11** 68 69

23°00'E Aberdeen 24°00'E

Swartberg Nat. Res.

Rooiloop
Ghwarriepoort
43

Barándas 20 12 14
R341 38 10
Buffelsklip
Nuwekloof
Studtis Sandvlakte
Baviaanskloof 30 45
Colekeplaas

**Kammanassieberge**
8 11
Potjiesberg Pass 13 9 Uniondale Zaaimansdal
Buffelsdrif Uniondale Poort
Molenrivier 13 18 Haarlem Misgund Kouga
Daskop 22 Louterwater
R 68 N 13 Die Vlug 1618m R 62
62 9 Speelmanskraal 1618m 19 Joubertina
Kleinplaat Prince Alfreds Pass 45 Heights Kouga
Bergplaas 28 R340 Bloukrans Formosa Kammiebos
Karatara Barrington The Pass Nat. Res.
Rondevlei Homtini Pass Crags 30 Stormsrivier
Phantom Wittedrift 15 Grootrivier Clarkson
Wilderness Pass **Knysna** 32 Pass T Woodlands
Sedgefield N Plettenberg TSITSIKAMMA Paul Sauer
2 Bay TOLL ROAD Bridge
*Walker Point* The Knysna National Cape Tsitsikamma
Heads Lake Area Seal National Park

DA

DB

SEE PAGES 54 - 55

*O c e a n*

DC

+ +

35°00'S

DD

DE

Copyright © Map Studio 2005

23°00'E 24°00'E

66 67 68 69

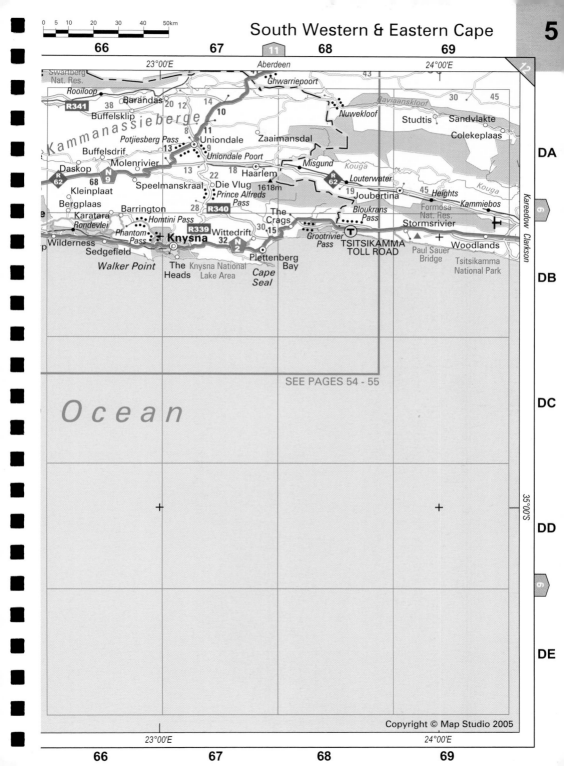

# Eastern Cape

Scale 1 : 1 500 000

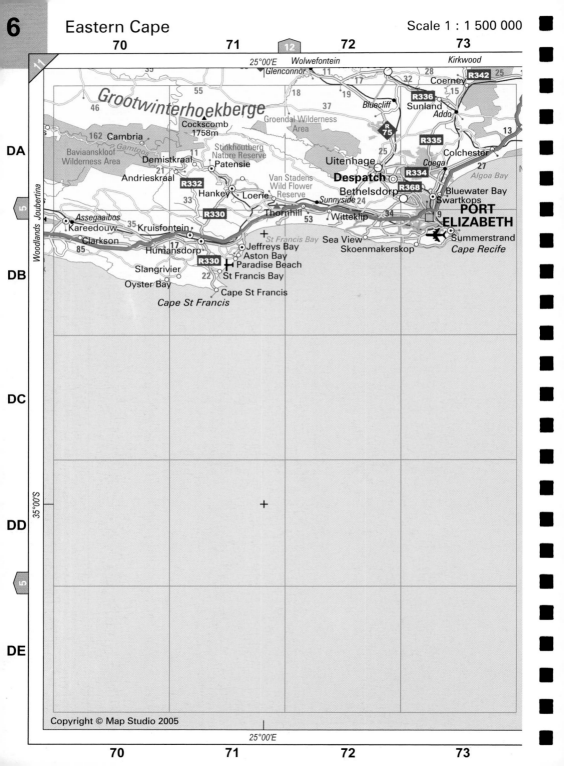

Copyright © Map Studio 2005

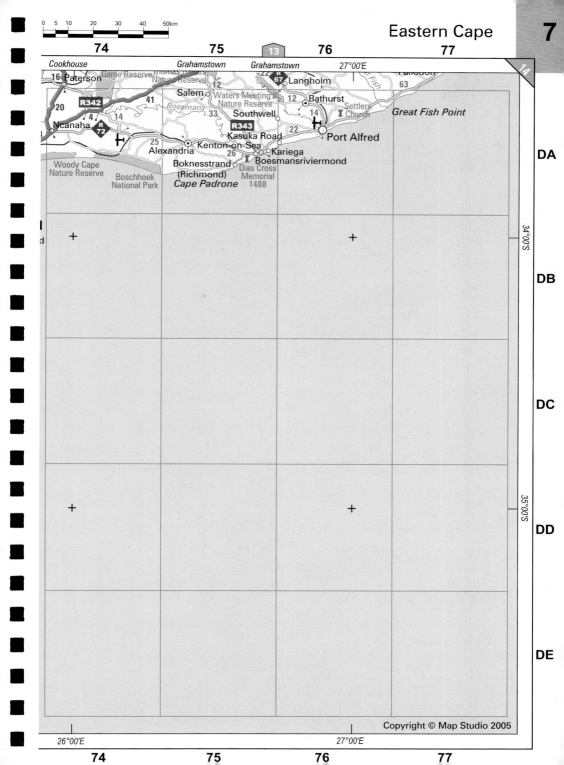

0 5 10  20  30  40  50km

Cookhouse        Grahamstown    Grahamstown    27°00'E        Palladon

16 Paterson    Game Reserve   Thomas Baines   Langholm    63
                Nature Reserve   67

20    R342    41    Salem    Waters Meeting    12 Bathurst
            Boesmans   Nature Reserve        Settlers
4   14    33    Southwell    14   Church    Great Fish Point
R72   Ncanaha        R343        22
                Kasuka Road        Port Alfred
        25    Kenton-on-Sea
Alexandria    26        Kariega    DA
Woody Cape   Boknesstrand    Dias Cross   Boesmansriviermond
Nature Reserve   (Richmond)   Memorial
    Boschhoek   Cape Padrone   1488
    National Park

34°00'S

+            +

DB

DC

35°00'S

+            +

DD

DE

Copyright © Map Studio 2005

26°00'E                27°00'E

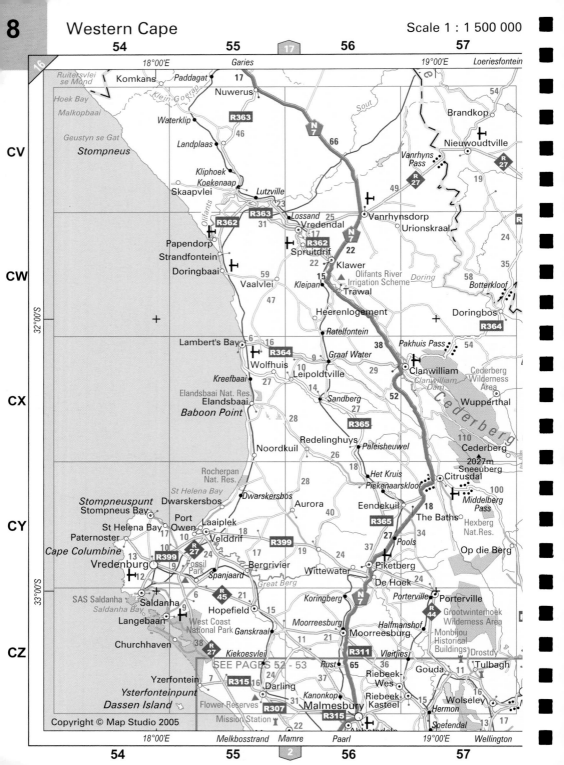

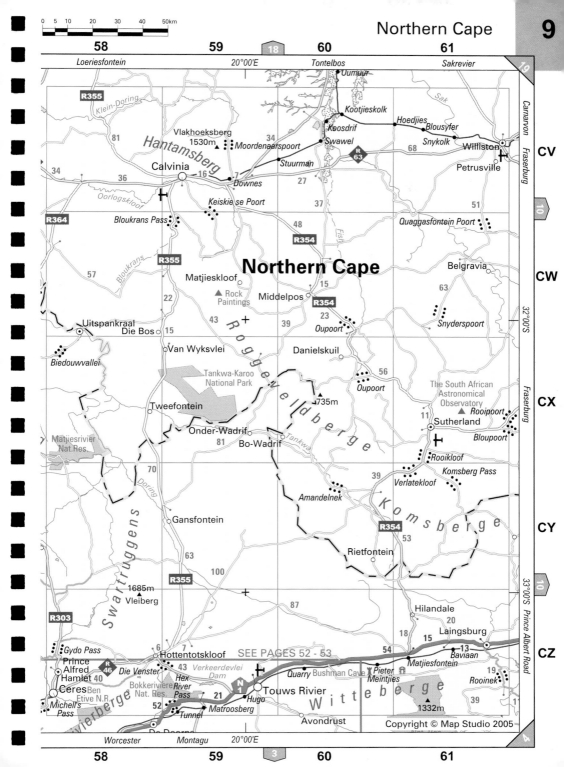

Loeriesfontein                    20°00'E          Tontelbos              Sakrevier

R355

Klein-Doring                                     Uumuur

81                                          Kootjieskolk         Hoedjies

Vlakhoeksberg          34        Koosdrif              Blousyfer
1530m          Moordenaarspoort       Swawel         Snykolk     Williston      **CV**

Hantamsberg                        Stuurman          R63       68

Calvinia    16                                                    Petrusville

34       36            7    Downes         27

Oorlogskloof                  Keiskie se Poort              37                 51

R364
Bloukrans Pass                              48            Quaggasfontein Poort

R354

57                                                                       Belgravia
R355                                                                              **CW**

Matjieskloof                    15                          63
Rock
Paintings      Middelpos    R354

22                   43       39       23
Oupoort

Uitspankraal                                                           Snyderspoort
Die Bos    15                        Danielskuil
Van Wyksvlei                                      56

Biedouwvallei                                                    The South African
Oupoort              Astronomical
Tankwa-Karoo                                      Observatory
National Park                 735m              11    Rooipoort            **CX**

Tweefontein                                          Sutherland

Onder-Wadrif                                              Bloupoort
81    Bo-Wadrif                                Rooikloof

70                                         39              Komsberg Pass
Verlatekloof

Gansfontein                    Amandelnek               Komsberg
63

100                                      R354
53
Rietfontein                                          **CY**

1685m
R355
Vleiberg                                                    Hilandale

87                          20
R303                                                               Laingsburg
Gydo Pass          6   7                                  18    15       13
Prince                Hottentotskloof    SEE PAGES 52 - 53          54           Baviaan
R46                                                          Matjiesfontein
Alfred   Die Venster   43   Verkeerdevlei
Hamlet 40                     Dam               Quarry Bushman Cave              19
Ceres  Bokkeriviere  Hex            N1         Pieter           Rooinek
Nat. Res.  River        Touws Rivier       Meintjies
Michell's           Pass    21   Hugo              Witteberge                 **CZ**
Pass         52      Matroosberg                             1332m       39
Tunnel                       Avondrust

Worcester    Montagu    20°00'E

**58**          **59**       3  **60**          **61**

Copyright © Map Studio 2005

Carnarvon  Fraserburg
10
32°00'S
Fraserburg
33°00'S  Prince Albert Road
10

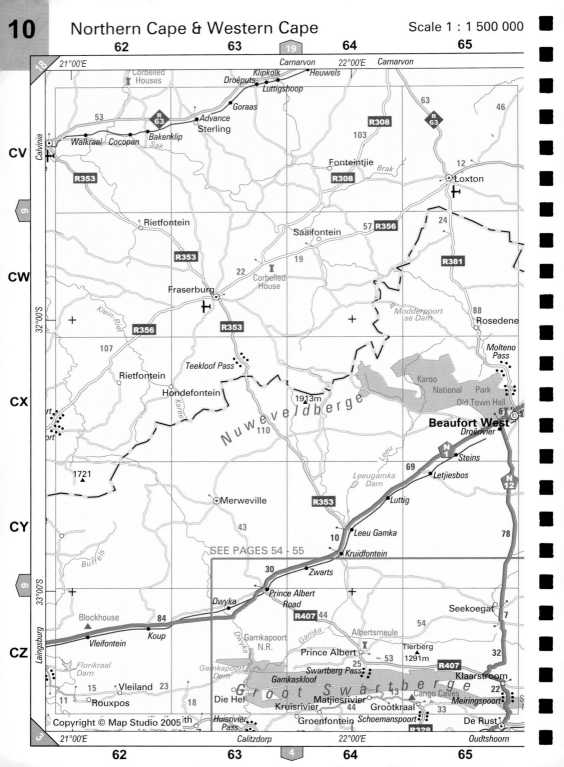

62    63    **19**    64    65

18

21°00'E    Carnarvon    22°00'E    Carnarvon

Corbelled Houses    Klipkolk    Heuwels
Droëputs    Luttigshoop
Goraas    63    46
53    Advance    R308    R63
Sterling    103
Walkraal  Cocopan  Bakenklip    12
Calvinia    Sak    Fonteintjie    Loxton
CV
R353    R308    Brak

9

Rietfontein    Saaifontein    57 R356    24
19    R381
R353    22
CW    Corbelled    88
Fraserburg    House    Modderpoort
se Dam    Rosedene
32°00'S    Klein-Riet    R356    R353    Molteno
107    Pass
Teekloof Pass    Karoo
Rietfontein    National    Park
CX    Hondefontein    1913m    Old Town Hall
ort    Nuweveldberge    Beaufort West
ort    110    Droërivier
1721    Leeu    Steins
N1    69    Letjiesbos
Leeugamka
Dam    N12
Merweville    R353    Luttig
CY    43    78
10    Leeu Gamka
SEE PAGES 54 - 55    Kruidfontein
Buffels    30    Zwarts
9    Dwyka    Prince Albert    Seekoegat
33°00'S    Road    7
Blockhouse    84    R407 44    54
Vleifontein    Koup    Albertsmeule    32
Laingsburg    Dwyka    Gamkapoort    25
CZ    Florikraal    N.R.    Prince Albert    Tierberg    R407
Dam    53    1291m    Klaarstroom
15  Vleiland  23    Gamkaskloof    Swartberg Pass    Cango Caves    22
11    18    Groot  Swartberge    13    Meiringspoort
Rouxpos    Die Hel    Matjiesrivier    Grootkraal    33
Huisrivier    Kruisrivier    44    De Rust
Copyright © Map Studio 2005    Pass    Groenfontein  Schoemanspoort    R328
21°00'E    Calitzdorp    22°00'E    Oudtshoorn

62    63    4    64    65

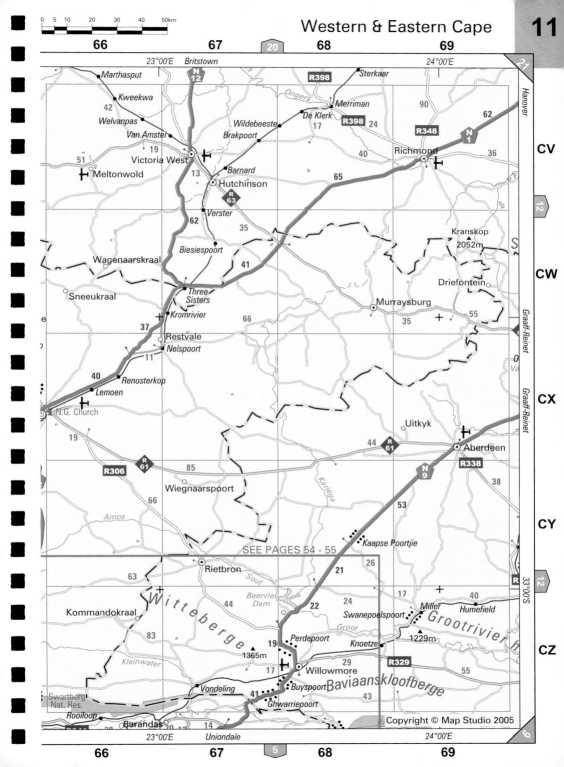

0  5  10    20    30    40    50km

23°00'E   Britstown                          24°00'E

Marthasput

Kweekwa

42

Welvanpas

Van Amstel

19

Meltonwold

51

Victoria West

13

Barnard

Hutchinson

63

Verster

62

35

Biesiespoort

41

Three Sisters

Kromrivier

37

66

Restvale

Nelspoort

11

40

Renosterkop

Lemoen

N.G. Church

19

R 61

R306          85

Wiegnaarspoort

66

Amos

SEE PAGES 54 - 55

Rietbron

63

Sout

Kommandokraal

Witteberge

44

Beervlei Dam

83

Kleinwater

Vondeling

41

Swartberg Nat. Res.

Rooiloop

Barandas

23°00'E   Uniondale

Sterkaar

R398

Merriman

De Klerk

R398   24

Wildebeeste

Brakpoort

17

90

R348

Richmond

N 1

62

40

36

65

Kranskop 2052m

Driefontein

Murraysburg

35

55

Uitkyk

44

R 61

Aberdeen

R338

N 9

38

53

Kaapse Poortjie

21          26

Groot

17          Miller

24          Humefield

40

22

Swanepoelspoort

Grootrivier

1229m

Perdepoort          Knoetze

19          29          R329

1365m

17          Willowmore

Buyspoort          43

Ghwarriepoort

Baviaanskloofberge

55

20          14

24°00'E

Hanover

CV

12

CW

Graaff-Reinet

CX

Graaff-Reinet

R 61

CY

33°00'S

12

CZ

Copyright © Map Studio 2005

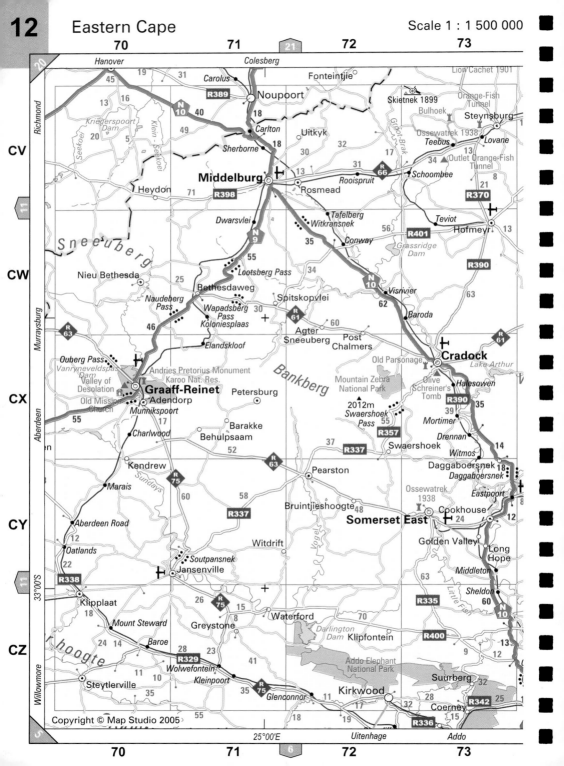

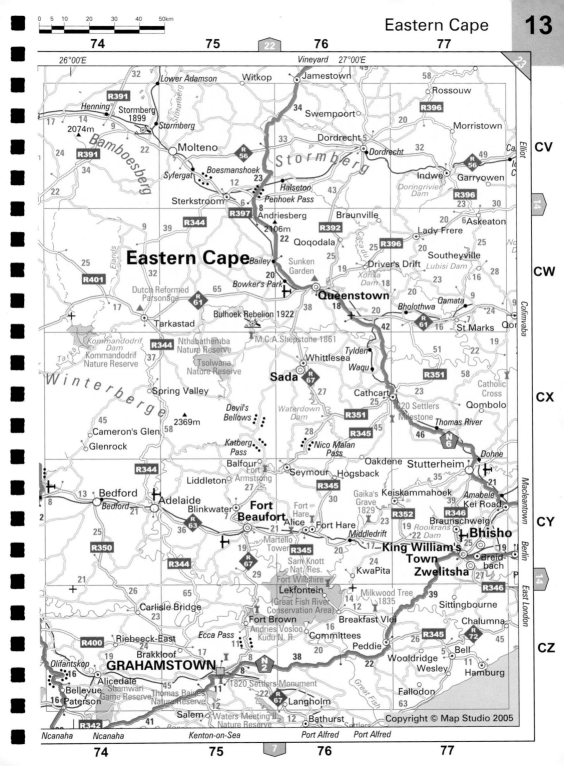

0 5 10 20 30 40 50km

**74** **75** **22** **76** **77**

Vineyard 27°00'E
26°00'E

23

32 Lower Adamson Witkop Jamestown 49

58

Henning R391 Rossouw
Stormberg Witkop 34 Swempoort Morristown R396 CV
1899 20
17 14 Stormberg Dordrecht 5
2074m Stormberg 33 Dordrecht 32 Indwe 49 Ca
Bamboesberg Molteno R 56 Garryowen R 56 Id
24 R391 22 23 Doringrivier 14 C
Halseton 43 Dam R396
34 Boesmanshoek 12 Penhoek Pass 23 30
22 Syfergat R397 8 Andriesberg Braunville 20 6 Askeaton
Sterkstroom 6 R344 2106m R392 Lady Frere Southeyville CW
R344 9 22 Qoqodala 20 6
39 Bailey Driver's Drift R396 23
**Eastern Cape** 25 Sunken 19 Lubisi Dam 16
R401 32 Garden Xonxa 25 23 24
25 20 Bowker's Park Dam 18 Qamata
65 Queenstown 20 Bholothwa 9
Dutch Reformed R 18 20 R 61 St Marks 24
Parsonage 61 42 16 Qon
17 Bulhoek Rebelion 1922 Tylden 51 19
Tarkastad M.C.A.Shepstone 1861 Whittlesea Waqu 58
Kommandodrif 37 R344 Tylden R351
Dam Nthabathemba Sada R Cathcart 23 CX
Kommandodrif Nature Reserve 67 27 20 Settlers
Nature Reserve Tsolwana 25 Milestone Qombolo
Winterberg Nature Reserve Waterdown 820 Settlers Thomas River
45 Spring Valley Dam Milestone 46 N 6 Dohne
Cameron's Glen 58 Devil's 28 R351 Oakdene Stutterheim 21
2369m Bellows Nico Malan R345 45 Hogsback 35
Glenrock Katberg Pass 30 Seymour Gaika's 39 Amabele CY
R344 Pass Balfour Fort R345 Grave Keiskammahoek Kei Road
13 Bedford Liddleton Armstrong 1829 23 R352 Braunschweig
8 Bedford Adelaide 27 Alice R346 Bhisho
2 Blinkwater R 21 Fort Fort Hare 19 Rooikrans 25
25 36 63 Martello Hare Middledrift 17 **King William's** 19
R350 Tower 20 **Town** Breid-
21 R344 R 67 Sam Knott KwaPita Zwelitsha bach P
26 65 Nat.Res. Milkwood Tree R346 CZ
Carlisle Bridge 29 Fort Willshire 14 1835 Sittingbourne
R400 Riebeeck-East Ecca Pass Lekfontein 12 Breakfast Vlei 39 Chalumna
19 Brakkloof 11 (Great Fish River 16 Committees R 72 45
Olifantskop 17 Conservation Area) 20 Peddie R345 Bell
**GRAHAMSTOWN** 8 Fort Brown 26 5
21 N Andries Vosloo Wooldridge Wesley 11 Hamburg
Alicedale 11 2 Kudu N.R. 22
Bellevue 45 1820 Settlers Monument 38 Fallodon
16 Paterson Shamwari 22 R 67 63
R342 Game Reserve Thomas Baines Langholm Great Fish
41 Nature Reserve Salem R
Waters Meeting 67
Ncanaha Ncanaha Kenton-on-Sea Nature Reserve Bathurst Copyright © Map Studio 2005
7 Port Alfred Port Alfred

**74** **75** **7** **76** **77**

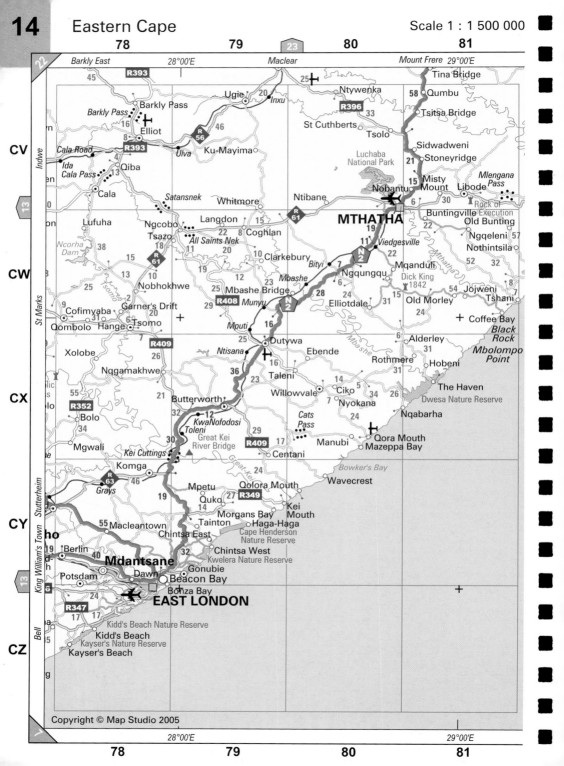

78    79    23    80    81

22

Barkly East    28°00'E    Maclear    Mount Frere   29°00'E

R393   45    25    Tina Bridge

Ntywenka   58   Qumbu

Ugie   20   Inxu

Barkly Pass    R396   33    Tsitsa Bridge

Barkly Pass    St Cuthberts    Tsolo

16   Elliot    R 56   46    Sidwadweni

**CV**    8   Cala Road   R393    Ulva   Ku-Mayima    Luchaba National Park   21   Stoneyridge

Ida   4   Qiba    Mlengana Pass

Indwe   Cala Pass   13    15   Misty Mount   Libode

Cala    Satansnek   Whitmore    Ntibane    Nobantu   6   30   Rock of

0    Lufuha    Langdon    R 61    **MTHATHA**   Buntingville Execution   Old Bunting

Ncora Dam   Ngcobo   22   8   Coghlan    19    22   Ngqeleni   57

Tsazo   All Saints Nek   11   Viedgesville    Nothintsila

38   18   11   20   Clarkebury   10    N 2   22   Mqanduli   52   32

**CW**   15   R 61   10   Nobhokhwe   19   12    Bityi   7   Ngqungqu    Dick King 1842   54   Jojweni

13   10    25   Mbashe Bridge   Mbashe   23   6   24   Old Morley   24   Tshani   7

25   2   Garner's Drift   29   R408   Munyu   28   Elliotdale   31    Coffee Bay

9   Cofimvaba   31   6   Tsomo    Mputi   16    Black Rock

Qombolo   Hange   7    R409    25   Dutywa   Ebende   6   Alderley   Mbolompo Point

Xolobe   26   Ntisana    16    Rothmere   31   Hobeni

Nqgamakhwe   36   23   Taleni    31

**CX**   55   R352   21   Butterworth    Willowvale   14   Ciko   34   26   The Haven    Dwesa Nature Reserve

Bolo   32   12   KwaNofodosi    7   Nyokana   24   Nqabarha

34   Toleni   30   Great Kei River Bridge   29   Cats Pass   Manubi   Qora Mouth

Mgwali   Kei Cuttings    R409   17   Centani    Mazeppa Bay

Komga    24    Bowker's Bay

R 63   46    Mpetu   Qolora Mouth   Wavecrest

Grays   19   Quko   27   R349

**CY**    14   Morgans Bay   Kei Mouth

ho   55   Macleantown   Tainton   Haga-Haga

19   Berlin   40   Chintsa East   Cape Henderson Nature Reserve

d-h    32   Chintsa West

Potsdam   **Mdantsane**   Dawn   Gonubie   Kwelera Nature Reserve

5   24   Beacon Bay

R347   17   17   Bonza Bay

**EAST LONDON**

Kidd's Beach Nature Reserve

a   Kidd's Beach

5   Kayser's Nature Reserve

**CZ**   Kayser's Beach

g

Copyright © Map Studio 2005

28°00'E    29°00'E

78    79    80    81

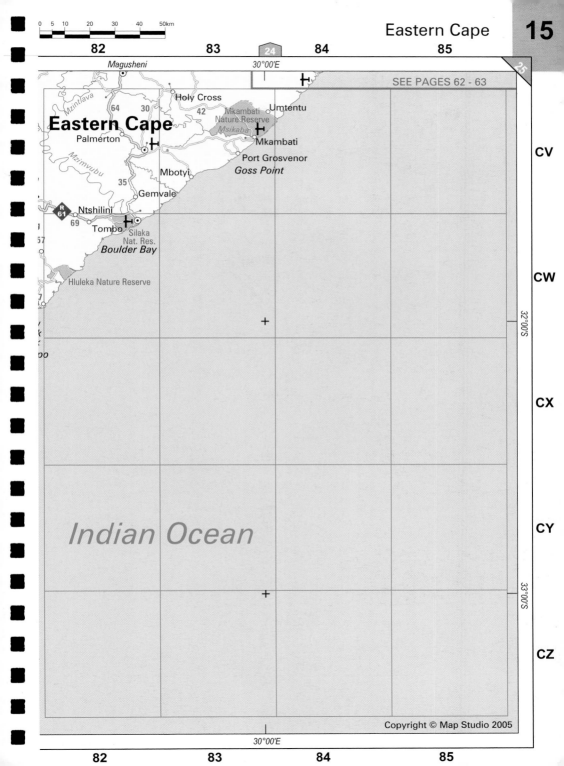

0 5 10 20 30 40 50km

82 83 24 84 85

Magusheni 30°00'E

SEE PAGES 62 - 63

Mzintlava 64 30 Holy Cross 42 Umtentu
Mkambati
Nature Reserve
**Eastern Cape** Msikaba Mkambati
Palmerton Port Grosvenor
*Goss Point*
Mzimvubu Mbotyi
35
Gemvale
R 61 Ntshilini
69 Tombo Silaka
Nat. Res.
*Boulder Bay*

Hluleka Nature Reserve

CV

CW

CX

*Indian Ocean*

CY

CZ

32°00'S

33°00'S

Copyright © Map Studio 2005

30°00'E

82 83 84 85

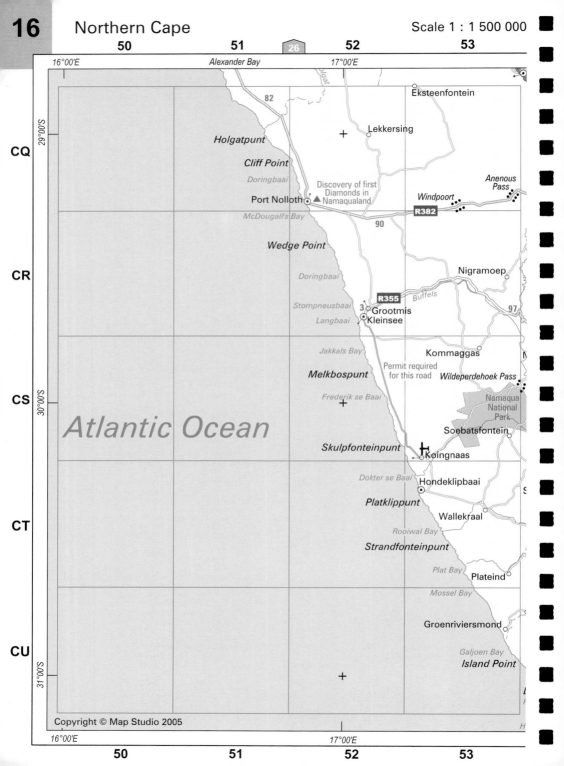

50    51    26    52    53

16°00'E    *Alexander Bay*    17°00'E

82

Eksteenfontein

29°00'S

CQ

Lekkersing

*Holgatpunt*

*Cliff Point*

*Doringbaai*

Discovery of first
Diamonds in
Namaqualand

*Anenous
Pass*

Port Nolloth    ▲    *Windpoort*

R382

*McDougall's Bay*

90

*Wedge Point*

Nigramoep

CR

*Doringbaai*

R355    *Buffels*

*Stompneusbaai*    3    Grootmis

97

*Langbaai*    Kleinsee

*Jakkals Bay*    Kommaggas

Permit required
for this road    *Wildeperdehoek Pass*

*Melkbospunt*

CS

30°00'S

# *Atlantic Ocean*

Namaqua
National
Park

Soebatsfontein

*Frederik se Baai*

*Skulpfonteinpunt*    ✈    Koingnaas

*Dokter se Baai*    Hondeklipbaai

CT

*Platklippunt*

Wallekraal

*Rooiwal Bay*

*Strandfonteinpunt*

*Plat Bay*    Plateind

*Mossel Bay*

Groenriviersmond

CU

*Galjoen Bay*

*Island Point*

31°00'S

Copyright © Map Studio 2005

16°00'E    17°00'E

50    51    52    53

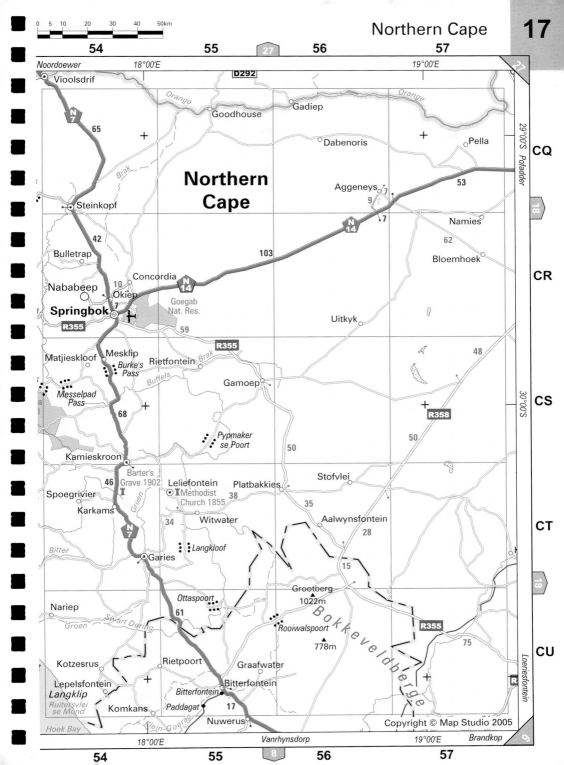

0 5 10 20 30 40 50km

54 55 27 56 57

Noordoewer 18°00'E 19°00'E 27

Vioolsdrif D292

N7 65 Orange Goodhouse Gadiep Orange

CQ 29°00'S Pofadder

Dabenoris Pella

**Northern Cape**

Aggeneys 7 53

9

Namies

Steinkopf N14 7

42 103 62

Bulletrap Bloemhoek CR

Concordia N14

Nababeep 10

Okiep Goegab

**Springbok** 7 Nat. Res.

R355 59 Uitkyk

Mesklip R355 Brak CR... 48

Matjieskloof Burke's Rietfontein

Pass

Messelpad Buffels Gamoep

Pass

68 CS 30°00'S

R358

Pypmaker

se Poort 50 50

Kamieskroon

Barter's Platbakkies Stofvlei

Grave 1902 Leliefontein

46 Methodist

Spoegrivier Church 1855 38 35 CT

Karkams 34 Witwater Aalwynsfontein

N7 28

Bitter Langkloof

15

Nariep Grootberg

Groen 1022m R355

61 Ottaspoort 75

Kotzesrus Rooiwalspoort

Rietpoort Graafwater 778m Bokkeveldberge CU

Lepelsfontein Bitterfontein

*Langklip* Bitterfontein

Ruitersvlei Komkans Paddagat 17

se Mond

Hoek Bay Nuwerus R

Copyright © Map Studio 2005

18°00'E Vanrhynsdorp 19°00'E Brandkop

54 55 8 56 57

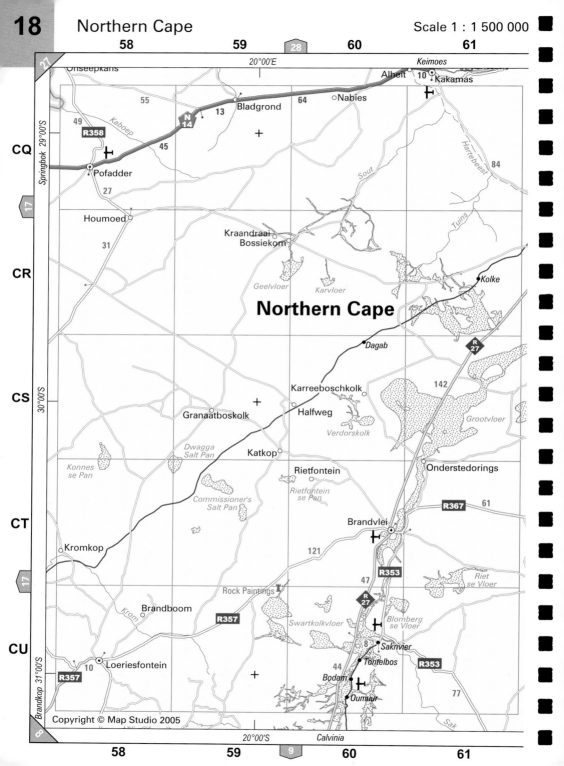

**Northern Cape**

Copyright © Map Studio 2005

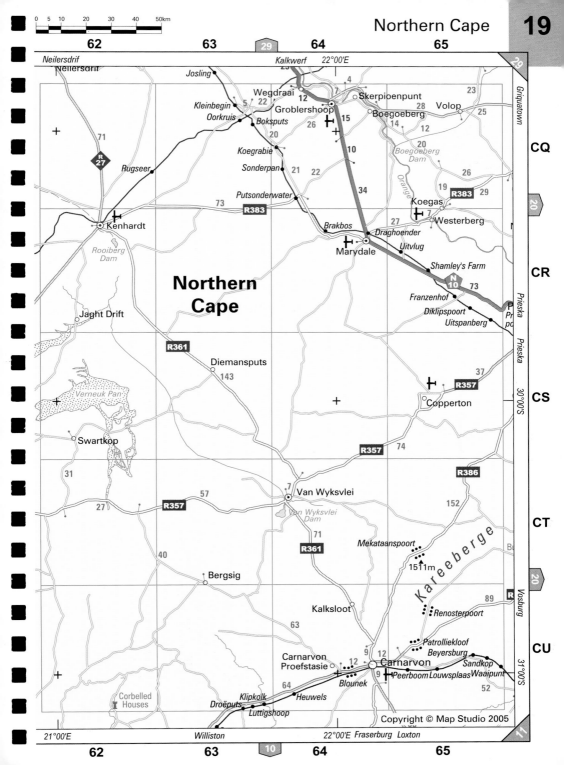

0 5 10 20 30 40 50km

**62** **63** 29 **64** **65**

Neilersdrif
Neilersdrif
Josling
Kalkwerf 22°00'E
29
Griquatown

Wegdraai 12
Kleinbegin 5 22
Oorkruis
Boksputs
20
Koegrabie
Sonderpan 21
Putsonderwater
R383
73
R383
Brakbos
Kenhardt
Rooiberg
Dam
Jaght Drift

4
7
Skerpioenpunt 23
Groblershoop 15
Boegoeberg 28 Volop
14 25
12
20
Boegoeberg
Dam
26
Koegas 19 R383 29
7 Westerberg
27
Draghoender
Uitvlug
Shamley's Farm
N
10 73
Franzenhof
Diklipspoort
Uitspanberg

CQ

CR

Orange

Priska
Priska
po

**Northern
Cape**

R361
Diemansputs
143

R357
Copperton 37
R357
74

Swartkop

Verneuk Pan

31

27
R357 57
Van Wyksvlei 7
Van Wyksvlei
Dam

R386

CS

CT

30°00'S

Vosburg
20

Kareeberge

152
Mekataanspoort
1511m
Renosterpoort 89

40
Bergsig

R361 71
Kalksloot
63

Patrolliekloof
Beyersburg
Carnarvon 12 12
Proefstasie
Blounek 64
Klipkolk Heuwels
Droëputs
Luttigshoop
Carnarvon
9 Peerboom Louwsplaas
Sandkop
Waaipunt
52

CU

31°00'S

Corbelled
Houses

21°00'E
Williston
22°00'E Fraserburg Loxton

10

Copyright © Map Studio 2005

**62** **63** 10 **64** **65**

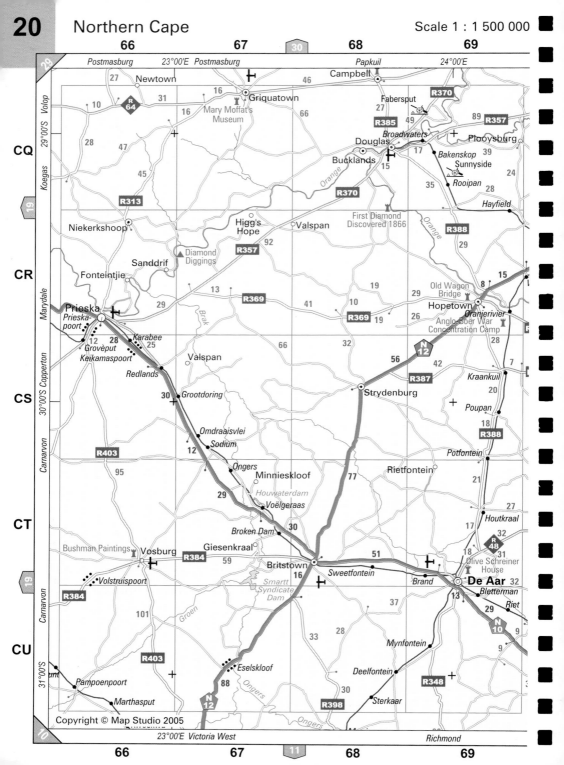

Copyright © Map Studio 2005

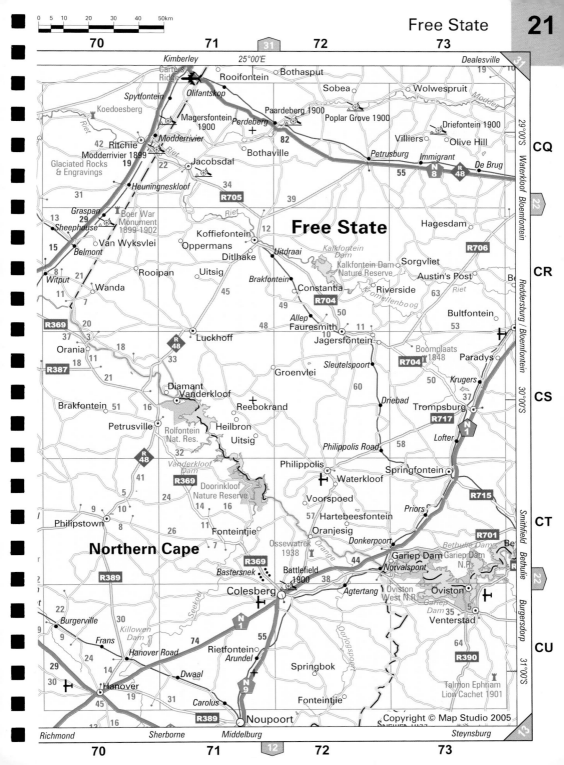

0 5 10   20   30   40   50km

Kimberley       25°00'E                Dealesville
19

Cartes Ridge
Rooifontein          Bothasput
Spytfontein                              Sobea          Wolwespruit
Olifantskop                                                          Modder
Koedoesberg          Magersfontein 1900   Paardeberg 1900   Poplar Grove 1900   Driefontein 1900
                     Perdeberg                                      Villiers   Olive Hill
42  Ritchie   Modderrivier                                                          29°00'S
Modderrivier 1899                      82                Petrusburg   Immigrant          **CQ**
19   22      Jacobsdal      Bothaville                              N8  R48  De Brug
Glaciated Rocks                                               55
& Engravings
31                                          34
Heuningneskloof               **R705**
39

Boer War                                                              Hagesdam
13  Graspan  Monument         Koffiefontein   12        **Free State**
29  1899-1902                                                                          22
Sheephouse              Oppermans              Kalkfontein
15                     Ditlhake      Uitdraai    Dam              Sorgvliet   **R706**
Belmont  Van Wyksvlei                           Kalkfontein Dam
                                                Nature Reserve   Austin's Post          **CR**
8   21      Rooipan    Uitsig      Brakfontein                                Riet
Witput                                          Constantia   Riverside   63        Be
11                                    49    **R704**
7   Wanda                         45        50                     Bultfontein
**R369**  20                              48   Allep   Fauresmith   11        53
37  3                          **R48**      10   Jagersfontein
Orania  18                    Luckhoff              Boomplaats          Paradys
18  11                    33            Groenvlei   1848     **R704**
**R387**       21                                  Sleutelspoort   50   Krugers   30°00'S
                    Diamant                      60              37      **CS**
Brakfontein  51  16  Vanderkloof              Driebad   Trompsburg
                    Reebokrand                              **R717**   N1
Petrusville        Heilbron                              Lofter
Rolfontein                    Uitsig                      58
Nat. Res.  32                         Philippolis Road
**R48**  41                                                  Springfontein
**R369**  Doorinkloof                Philippolis                          **R715**   22
Vanderkloof    Nature Reserve        Waterkloof
Dam                                   Voorspoed      Priors
5   24        16                    57  Hartebeesfontein                    **CT**
9   10                    11  Fonteintjie   Oranjesig                      **R701**
Philipstown  8              26        7        Donkerpoort   44        **Bethulie Dams**   Be
**Northern Cape**                Ossewatrek              Gariep Dam  Gariep Dam
R389                          1938    Battlefield  38  Norvalspont   N.P.        R
                    Bastersnek            1900                                          22
22        30      Colesberg        Agtertang  Oviston   Oviston
Burgerville  Killowen                          West N.R.
9   9      Frans  Dam      74        55                          Gariep  35
24              Hanover Road   Rietfontein                  Dam   Venterstad   **CU**
29  14        Dwaal  Arundel                  64
30              N9      Springbok              **R390**
Hanover  19   31   Carolus            Fonteintjie   Talmon Ephriam
45  16                                          Lion Cachet 1901

Copyright © Map Studio 2005

Richmond       Sherborne    Middelburg              Steynsburg

74    75    32    76    77

26°00'E Soutpan    Brandfort    Winburg    Winburg    Marquard

37

10    Florisbad    Alleman    50    8    Flora    R706

Lumsden's Horse
R30    Karee    Monument 1900    Verkeerdevlei    31    Excelsior    55    R703

Krugersdrif
Dam    Soetdoring    Glen    N1    Sediba    Rakhoi    Rock Paintings    Modderpoort    37
Nat. Res.    R64

29°00'S

28    Brandwag    Maselspoort    Mockes Dam    Spitskop    37    Westminster    Ladybrand

**CQ**    Raasaai    7    **BLOEMFONTEIN**    Paradys
Shannon    59    Sepane    Tweespruit    20    Marseilles    11
28    Woman's    Sannaspos    N8    33    16
Monument    Rodenbeck    Thaba Nchu    Frankfort
Waterkloof    Ferreira    **Botshabelo**    Maseru

21    38    Thaba Phatshwa    Bridge

Jagersfontein    60    Rustfontein Dam    Leeurivier Dam    Kommissiepoort    **MASERU**
Tierpoort    Rustfontein Dam    R709    44    R26    23
Dam    Nature Reserve    40    Mazenod
Tierpoort    71    Uysklip    Hobhouse    27
Bethania    R702    Meadows    Caledon    59

**CR**    109    Dewetsdorp    Morija
Reddersburg    R717    36    Nevada    8    Wepener    A2

Riet    52    Jammerdrif    8    A20
Fouriespruit    24    Caledon    Van Rooyens    25    Mafeteng
R717    Nat. Res.    Gate    Rock
Edenburg    70    Helvetia    Welbedacht    Dereham    R26    Paintings
Dam    Birdpark    35

**CS**    Gomvlei    Gen. de Wet's    Vanstadensrus    Sepapus Gate    Cannibal
Birthplace    Gelukwaarts    Egmont    Caves
Breipaal    76    R701    Dam    Boesmanskop    Mohales Hoek
Slyk    Caledon    62    Makhalengbrug
Rubida

Smithfield    35    Klipplaatsdrif 1839    Zastron    A2
Dupleston    R701    29    Palmietfontein
66    Genadeberg    R726    40
Louw    Tussen-die-Riviere    Rouxville    25
Wepener    Game Farm    Uitsig    Koukraal    Bildemar    Leeubank    R726 R393

**CT**    Pellissier House    Goedemoed    Anglo-    Sterkspruit
Bethulie    Museum    Hot    Boer War    R392    Bluegums
R390    Olive    Sulphur    Monument    53    Herschel
Springs    Brughalte    30    34

21    Orange    Masango    Lady Grey
Knapdaar    56    Braamspruit    48    R58    Bamboeskloof
Ontspringen    Beerley    Karringmelkspruit    New
R58    Lekkerdraai    27    Vickers    England
Osfontein    Vineyard    N6    23    Motkop    33

**CU**    Taalmonument    54    Clanville    9
Burgersdorp    Jamestown    R392    Clifford
32    Lower Adamson    Witkop    49    58    Rossouw

Copyright © Map Studio 2005

26°00'E Steynsburg    Queenstown    27°00'E    Morristown

74    75    13    76    77

Copyright © Map Studio 2005

Scale 1 : 1 500 000

**82**     **83**     34     **84**     **85**

Bergville / Ladysmith  Van Reenen  Colenso  30°00'E

Blockhouse
Zunckels  22  Winterton
Mike's Pass  17  Chieveley  30  67  The Ranch
Loskop  Frere  Bloukrans  Weenen  Keate's Drift
Ntabamhlope  50  Monument  Weenen  Muden  General  22
  Estcourt  Game  62  Louis Botha's
**CQ**  South Downs  Saailaen  Reserve  Greytown  Birthplace 1862  34
R600  Mvozana  Ahrens
Rockmount  Mooi River  Craigie  R622  56
Burn Dam  Mount Alida  Sevenoaks
R74  67  Karkloof  R33
Rosetta  Stanmore  MIDLANDS TOLL ROUTE  Nature Reserve  Dalton  Fawnleas
Redcliffe  N3  York  New Hanover
Nottingham Road  46  Albert Falls  Mpolweni  Wartburg  R614
Balgowan  Nature Reserve  Albert Falls
uKhahlamba  Lidgetton  **Howick**  Valley of
Drakensberg Park  Midmar Nat. Res.  Merrivale  14  1000 Hills
(World Heritage Site)  Midmar  16  **PIETERMARITZBURG**
Lower Loteni  Dam  Hilton  Colenso
Sani Pass  iMpendle  Queen Elizabeth Park  18  Mission
Sani Pass  73  **Edendale**  Station 1854
Munywini  Ashburton  Camperdown
Himeville  32  Thornville  65
Nature  Hammersdale
Himeville  Reserve  **Mpumalanga**
Underberg  Woodford  Butu  uMhlongonek  20  **MARIANNHILL**
R617  Deholm  R617  Bulwer  Richmond  R624  45
80  Coleford  32  Rosebank  32  R603
Nat. Res.  Donnybrook
Coleford  uMbumbulu
SEE PAGE 60 - 61  Adams Mission
Kingscote  Creighton  Mkomazi  42  R56  iXopo  uMgababa
Riverside  Bush  Dududu  42
Reserve  35  uMkomaas
Dulini  C.J. Rhodes'  Clansthal
Swartberg  Sneezewood  House  Vernon Crookes
Singisi  Umzimkulu  Nature Reserve  Scottburgh
Franklin  Highflats  74  Braemar  Park
Bailden  **Eastern Cape**  uMzinto  Rynie
45  Mount Currie  Bontrand  Kelso
Nat. Res.  Bisi  Goba  Pennington
Boy Scout  Klipspruit  38  Sezela
War Memorial  Stafford's Post  R102  Bazley
Kokstad  Karg's Post  36  17  Harding  St Faith's  KwaDweshula  N2  iFafa Beach
Bonny  Weza  67  47  Mthwalume
Ridge  4  Turton
Brooks Nek  8  Oribi Gorge  Hibberdene
20  28  Nat. Res.  uMzumbe
11  Fort Donald  Ngabeni  N2  Southport
Mount Ayliff  R61  Izingolweni  Paddock  Marburg  N2  Sea Park
Magusheni  30  Bizana  Port Shepstone  uMtentweni
Ngabeni  SOUTH COAST  22  R620  Shelly Beach
Ntabankulu  R61  Redoubt  TOLL ROAD  T  uVongo
17  38  53  Southbroom  Margate
35  Munster  20  R61  Ramsgate
R61  49  Palm Beach
Flagstaff  Umtamvuna Nat. Res.  Glenmore Beach
Banner Rest
Copyright © Map Studio 2005  Holy Cross  Port Edward
SEE PAGES 62 - 63

Palmerton  30°00'E

**82**     **83**     15     **84**     **85**

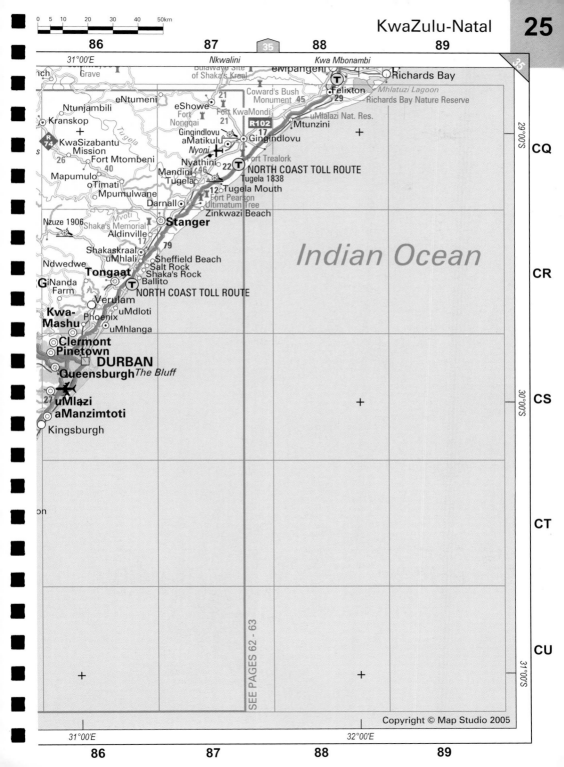

0 5 10 20 30 40 50km

86 87 35 88 89

31°00'E   Nkwalini   Kwa Mbonambi

Grave
of Shaka's Kraal
eMpangeni ○Richards Bay
Coward's Bush ⊤Felixton Mhlatuzi Lagoon
eNtumeni Monument 45 29 Richards Bay Nature Reserve
Ntunjambili 21 uMlalazi Nat. Res.
eShowe 21
○Kranskop Fort 17 Mtunzini
Nongqai R102 +
KwaSizabantu Gingindlovu
Mission aMatikulu ○Gingindlovu
26 Fort Mtombeni Nyoni Fort Trealork
40 Nyathini 22 ⊤ NORTH COAST TOLL ROUTE
Mapumulo Mandini (46) Tugela 1838
oTimati Tugela Tugela Mouth
Mpumulwane 12 Fort Pearson
Darnall○ Ultimatum Tree
Mvoti Zinkwazi Beach
Nzuze 1906 Shaka's Memorial ○○Stanger
Aldinville○ Indian Ocean +
Shakaskraal 79
Ndwedwe uMhlali Sheffield Beach CR
Tongaat○ Salt Rock
G○Nanda ○Shaka's Rock
Farm ⊤ ○Ballito
Verulam○ NORTH COAST TOLL ROUTE
Kwa- Phoenix○ ○uMdloti
Mashu○ ○uMhlanga
○Clermont
○Pinetown
DURBAN
○Queensburgh The Bluff
27○ uMlazi +
aManzimtoti CS
○ Kingsburgh

29°00'S CQ

30°00'S

SEE PAGES 62 - 63

CT

+ +

CU

31°00'S

31°00'E 32°00'E

86 87 88 89

Copyright © Map Studio 2005

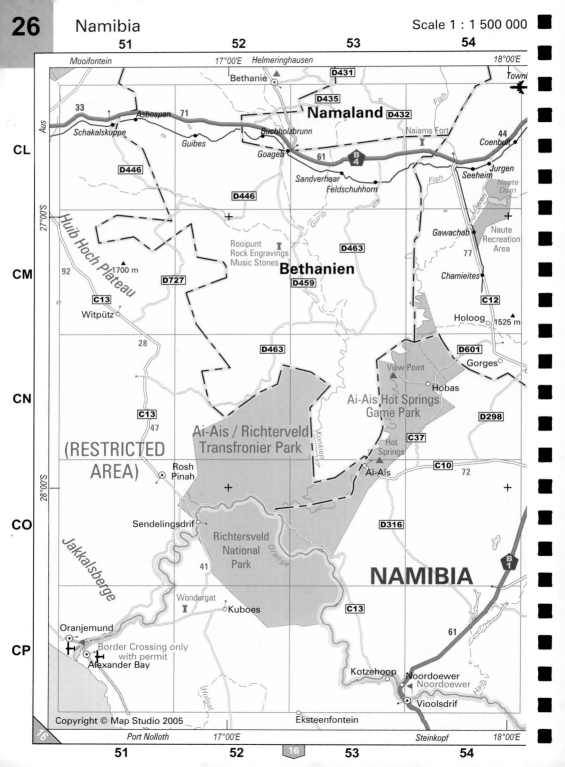

**51**  **52**  **53**  **54**

Mooifontein   17°00'E   Helmeringhausen   18°00'E

Bethanie   **D431**   Town

**D435**   **Namaland**   **D432**

Aus   33   Asbospan   71   Buchholzbrunn   Naiams Fort   44

Schakalskuppe   Guibes   Goageb   61   **B4**   Coenbult

**CL**

Sandverhaar   **B4**   Seeheim   Jurgen

**D446**   Feldschuhhorn   Fish   Naute Dam

**D446**   Gurib

27°00'S   Gawachab   Naute Recreation Area

Huib Hoch Plateau   Rooipunt Rock Engravings Music Stones   **D463**   77

92   1700 m   **D727**   **Bethanien**   Chamieites

**CM**   **D459**   **C12**

**C13**   Holoog   1525 m

Witpütz   **D601**

28   View Point   Gorges

**D463**   Hobas

**CN**   Ai-Ais Hot Springs Game Park   **D298**

**C13**   **Ai-Ais / Richterveld Transfronier Park**   Konkiep   **C37**

47   Hot Springs

**(RESTRICTED**   Rosh Pinah   Ai-Ais   **C10**   72

**AREA)**

28°00'S

**CO**   Sendelingsdrif   **D316**

Jakkalsberge   **Richtersveld National Park**   Orange   **NAMIBIA**   **B1**

41

Wondergat   Kuboes   **C13**   61

Oranjemund

**CP**   Border Crossing only with permit   Kotzehoop   Noordoewer

Alexander Bay   Noordoewer

Holgat   Vioolsdrif

Copyright © Map Studio 2005

16   Port Nolloth   17°00'E   Steinkopf   18°00'E

Eksteenfontein

**51**  **52**  16  **53**  **54**

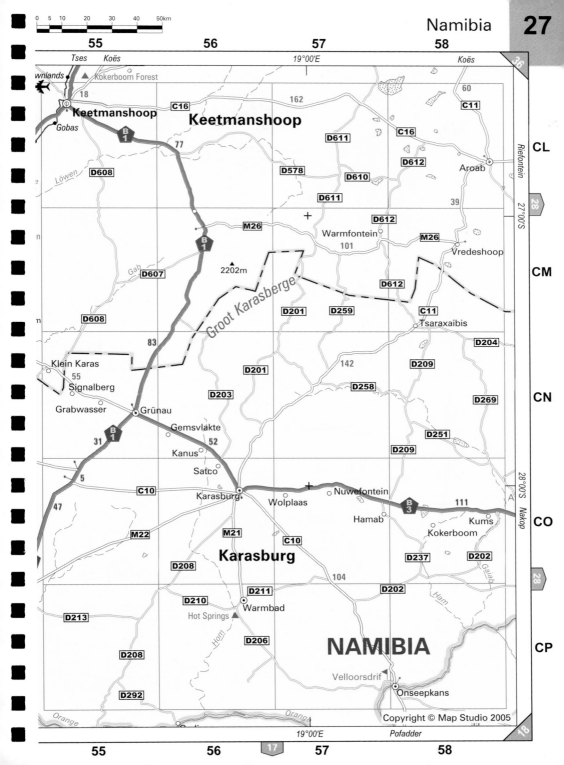

0 5 10 20 30 40 50km

| 55 | 56 | 57 | 58 |

*Tses*   *Koës*                    19°00'E                    *Koës*

36

*wnlands* ▲ Kokerboom Forest                                   60

18                    **C16**                    162          **C11**

**Keetmanshoop**          **Keetmanshoop**          **C16**

*Gobas*          **B1**                    **D611**          **C16**

**CL**

**D608**          **D578**          **D612**          Aroab

Riefontein   27°00'S   **28**

*Löwen*          **D610**

**D611**                    39

*Gab*          **M26**                    **D612**

**B1**          Warmfontein          **M26**

**D607**          101          Vredeshoop

▲ 2202m          Groot Karasberge

**CM**

**D608**                    **D612**

83          **D201**   **D259**          **C11**

Tsaraxaibis

**D204**

Klein Karas          **D201**          142          **D209**

55          Signalberg

**D203**          **D258**          **D269**

**CN**

Grabwasser          Grünau

Gemsvlakte          52          **D251**

**B1**          Kanus

31          Satco          **D209**

5          **C10**          Nuwefontein

Karasburg          Wolplaas          **B3**          111          Kums

47          Hamab          Kokerboom

28°00'S   Nakop   **CO**

**M22**          **M21**          **C10**          **D237**   **D202**

**Karasburg**          Gaiab

**D208**          104          **D202**

**28**

**D210**   **D211**

**D213**          Warmbad

Hot Springs ▲          *Ham*

*Hom*          **D206**

**NAMIBIA**

**CP**

**D208**          Velloorsdrif ▶

**D292**          Onseepkans

*Orange*          *Orange*          Copyright © Map Studio 2005

18

19°00'E          *Pofadder*

**17**

| 55 | 56 | 57 | 58 |

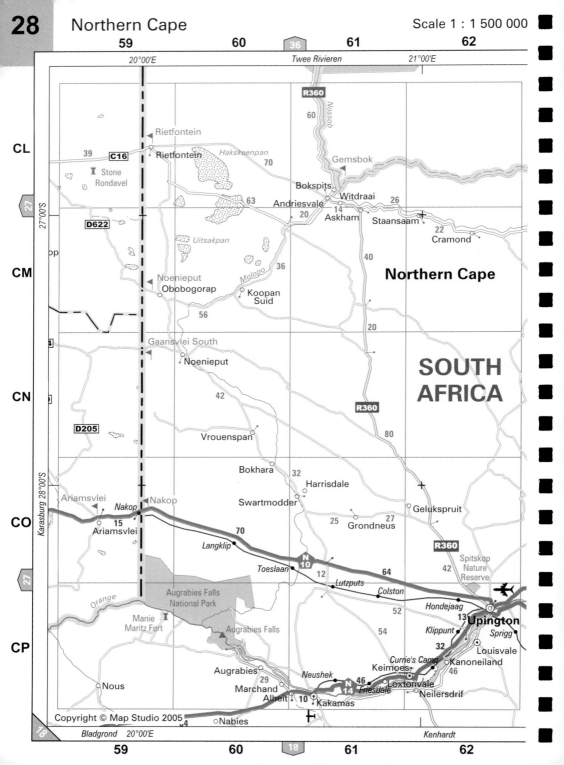

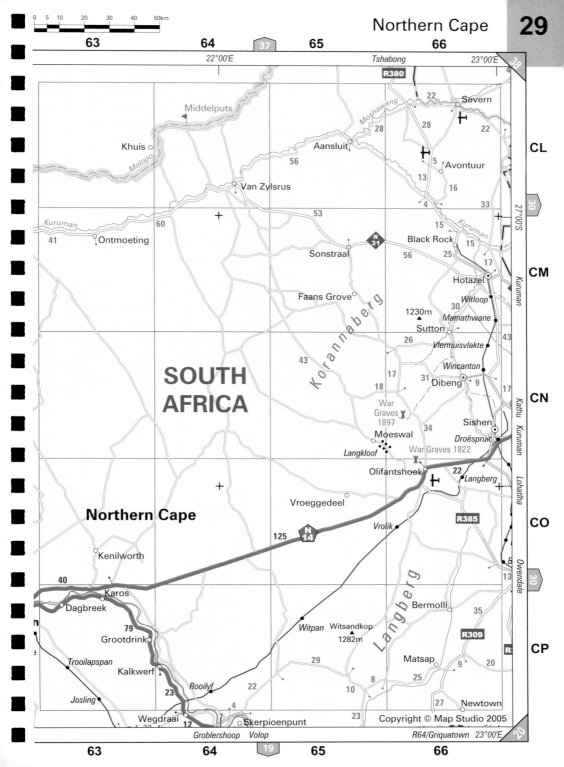

0 5 10 20 30 40 50km

**63** 64 65 **66**

22°00'E    Tshabong    23°00'E

R380

Severn    **CL**

Middelputs    22
28    28    22

Khuis    Aansluit    5    Avontuur

56    13    16

Van Zylsrus    4    33

Molopo

Kuruman    53    15    Kuruman    27°00'S

60    41    Ontmoeting    15    Black Rock    15    **CM**

R31    56    25

Sonstraal    17

Hotazel

Faans Grove    Witloop

30    Mamathwane
1230m    Sutton    26    Vlermuisvlakte    43

43    Wincanton    **CN**

17    31    Dibeng    9
18    17

**SOUTH**    War    Graves    1897    34    Sishen
**AFRICA**    Moeswal    Droëspruit
Langkloof    War Graves 1822

Olifantshoek    22    Langberg

Vroeggedeel    **CO**

**Northern Cape**    Vrolik    R385

125    N14    13

Kenilworth

40    Karos    Bermolli    35    **CP**

Dagbreek

79    Witpan    Witsandkop    Matsap    9    20
Grootdrink    1282m    25

Trooilapspan    29    8    10

Kalkwerf    Rooilyf    22    23

23    4    27    Newtown

Josling    Wegdraai    Skerpioenpunt    23    Copyright © Map Studio 2005

12

Groblershoop    Volop    R64/Griquatown 23°00'E

**63** 64 65 **66**

67 68 38 69 70

37
24°00'E Crafthole

47
24
23
Tlhakgameng

23

Kgokgole
Ganyesa
23
56

30
20
36 Alettesrus

**North West**
3
37
R378 Setuat

CL
14
35
Coetzersdam
32
21

Maswehatshe
Louwna

Moshaweng

Ditshipeng
27°00'S

Geluk

Bothithong
Takoon 1823
69
Korobela

Tsineng
46

57

N14

Ga-Mopedi
Moffatt's Mission Church
Lykso

CM
Mathwaring
58

R31
Seoding
1833
Steekdorings
Salpeterpan

59
Mothibistad
R371
23

43
13
51
44

Kuruman
12
34
Reivilo
55
R372

Eye of Kuruman
19
R372
The Taung Skull

N14
47
14
16
23

CN
Kathu
41
Bekker
21
Blesmanspos
47

16
Gakarosa
Blikfontein
14

Madipelesa
1855m
20
23
R373
Espagsdrif
Boetsap

Mookaneng
Wonderwerk Caves
21

Spitskop Dam
Harts
11

Lohatlha
Beaconsfield

Glosam
25
Mount Rupert
18

CO
Palingpan
Daniëlskuil
12
Koopmansfontein
R370
Gordonia

Bokkoppie
10
38
R31
12
Ulco
30
Riviera

Beeshoek
Blinkklip
Owendale
Plateau
Kneukel
34
7
Elandsdrift
31

15
R385
38
Ariesfontein
Silver Streams

13
Postmasburg
Silver Streams
Lime Acres
Sydney-on-Vaal
Delportshoop
R375

38
30
R370
Winter's Rush
Longlands
St Mary's Anglican Church

**Asbesberge**
Papkuil
49
Vaalbos National Park
31
**Barkly West**

CP
R325
Rietfontein
42
Archaeological Reserve
Fieldsview
49

Koegelbeen Caves
R385
27 Livingstone Church
30
6
Schmidtsdrif
R64
68

28
46
Campbell

Copyright © Map Studio 2005
Fabersput
R370
Spytfontein

20
Griquatown
Douglas Douglas 24°00'E
Douglas

67 68 20 69 70

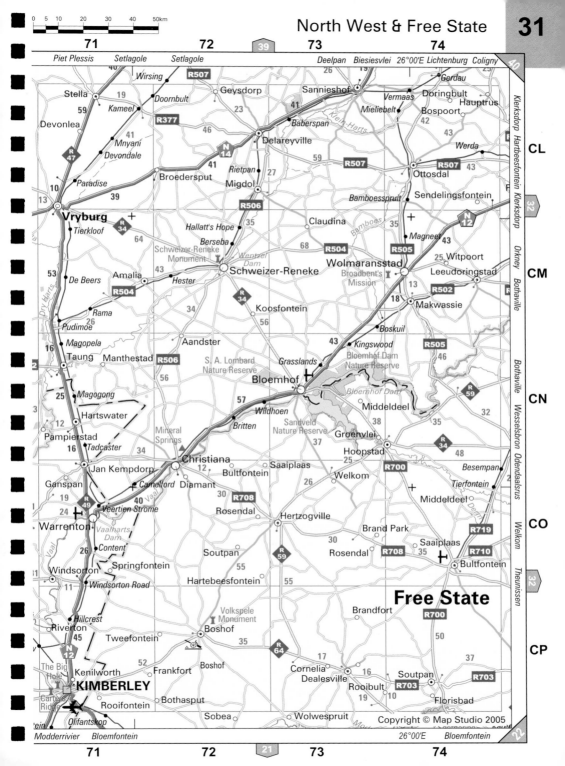

75    76    40    77    78

Ventersdorp   27°00'S   Carletonville   Lenasia   Johannesburg

Niesa   R501   Walkerville

Hauptrus

R30   55   56   41   Danie Theron Monument   28   **Sebokeng**   R82   14

29   Brakspruit   R53   21   R54   **Vereeniging**   **Vanderbijlpark**

R503   22   11   35   R500   **Sasolburg**

**CL**

22   New Machavie   45   N12   **POTCHEFSTROOM**   Venterskroon   19   59   20   13

**KLERKSDORP**   **Stilfontein**   48   R53   **KROONVAAL TOLL ROUTE**   Wolwehoek

6   Renosterspruit   13   **Parys**   14   T

Ottosdal

33   **Orkney**   22   26   53

Wolmaransstad

23   R502   10   29   Reitzburg   39   16   Dover   R82   R57

32   R76   10   Spes Bona   R720   20   N1   40

Harrisburg   Oasis   75   26   14   35

**CM**

19   R30   39   **Viljoenskroon**   Groenebloem   7   Koppies Dam

Leeudoring

Vaal   Mirage   38   R721   R723

R504   R59   34   55   33   36

**Bothaville**   48   Rustig   R727

Doornkraal Memorial   18   Vals   Heuningspruit   R720   Battle of Vechtkop

Schuttesdraai   29   R76   26   6   40

58   R713   Westleigh   R34

Hoopstad

R719   25   47   **Maokeng**   42   Prehistoric Stone Huts

Ancona   R30   **Kroonstad**   20   R725

**CN**

Prospectors Borehole Monument   49   R34   R76   48   27   R720   32

Hoopstad

**Odendaalsrus**   Kutlwanong   Geneva   50   Wonderkop   25   Allemansnek

15   R34   31   Riebeeckstad   36   R76   R707

24   **WELKOM**   Thabong   **Hennenman**   Komspruit   Arlington

Whites   18

28°00'S

**Virginia**   R73   Ooreenkoms

**CO**

Sand   48   R720   R707   Libertas

Welgeleë   Parys   Sand River Convention 1852   R70   Biddulph

R30   23   49   43   Allemanskraal Dam   25   8

Bultfontein

31

Theron   Willem Pretorius Game Reserve   54   **Senekal**   27

R708   60   N1   N5   R707   72

**Theunissen**   R708   31   11   Montevideo

Deelspruit   10   Erfenis Dam   43   Panorama

42   6   **Winburg**   Voortrekker Monument   R708

**CP**

Eensgevonden   49   43   Marquard

Houtenbeck   14   R73   31   R70

Soutpan

35   **Brandfort**   R703   53   R709   Flora   R708   Generaalsn

R30   Alleman   50   8   Witteberge

Copyright © Map Studio 2005

Gumtree

Bloemfontein   Excelsior   Excelsior   Clocolan   Ficksburg

75    76    22    77    78

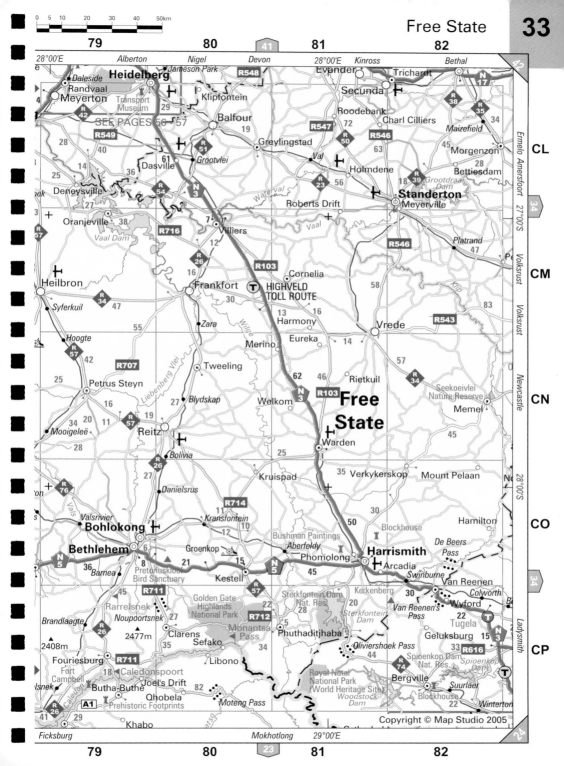

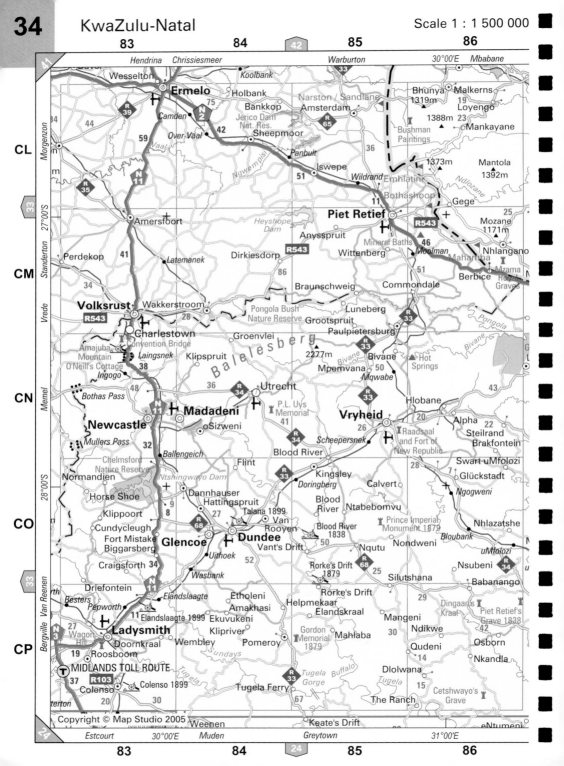

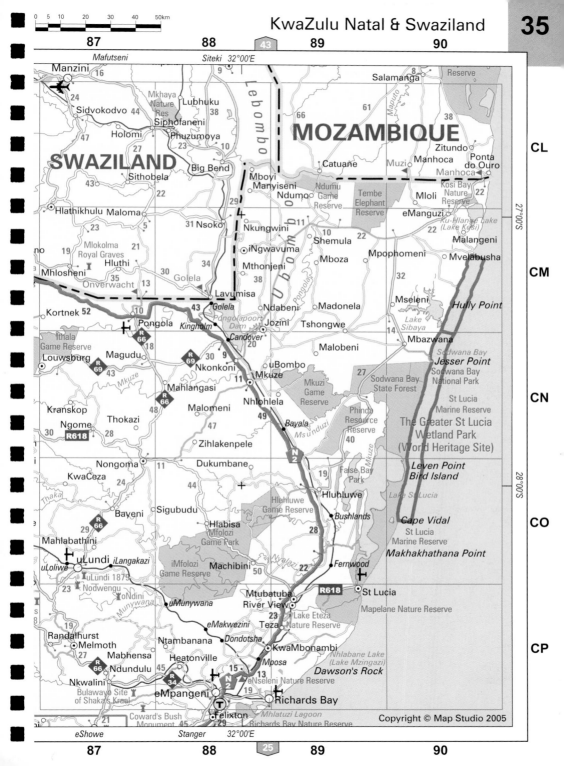

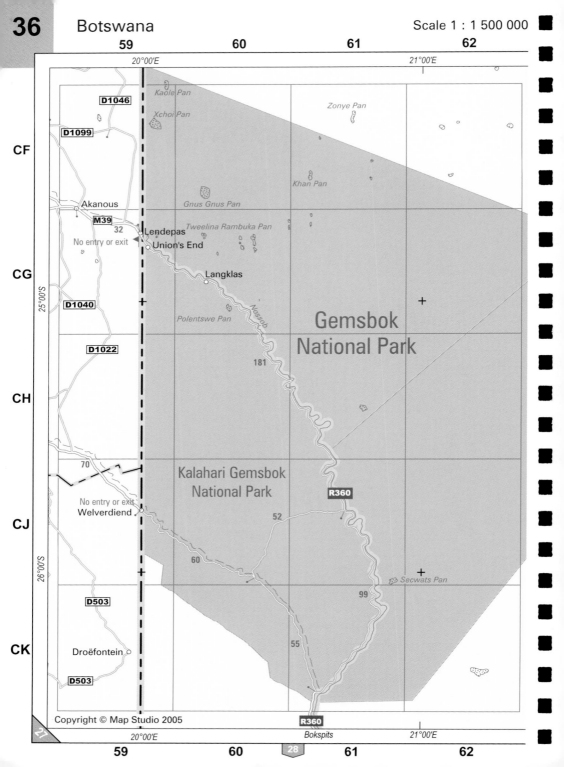

**59**    **60**    **61**    **62**

20°00'E    21°00'E

D1046

D1099

Kaole Pan

Xchoi Pan

Zonye Pan

CF

Khan Pan

Gnus Gnus Pan

Akanous

M39

32

Tweelina Rambuka Pan

Lendepas

No entry or exit

Union's End

CG

Langklas

25°00'S

D1040

Polentswe Pan

Nossob

D1022

181

Gemsbok
National Park

CH

70

Kalahari Gemsbok
National Park

No entry or exit

Welverdiend

R360

CJ

52

26°00'S

60

Secwats Pan

D503

99

CK

Droëfontein

55

D503

Copyright © Map Studio 2005

R360

Bokspits

20°00'E    21°00'E

**59**    **60**    **61**    **62**

27

28

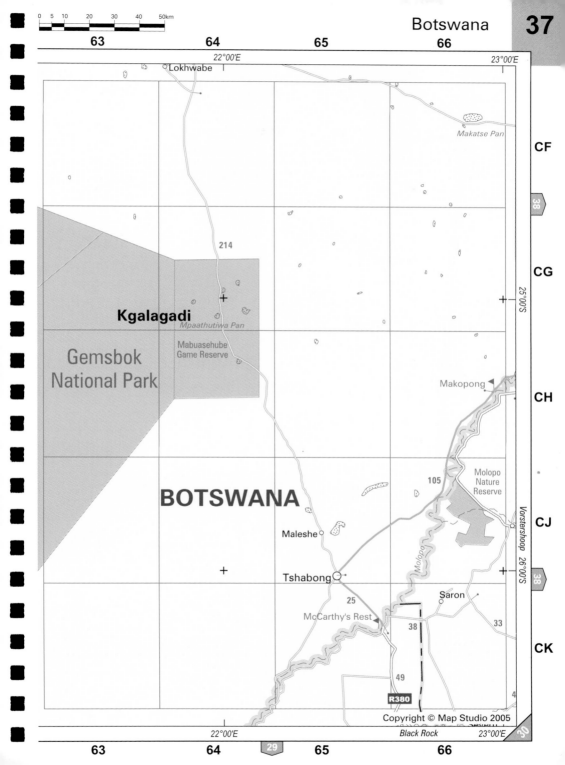

0 5 10 20 30 40 50km

63   64   65   66

22°00'E   23°00'E

Lokhwabe

Makatse Pan

CF

38

214

CG   25°00'S

Kgalagadi

Mpaathutiwa Pan

Mabuasehube
Game Reserve

Gemsbok
National Park

Makopong

CH

Molopo
Nature
Reserve

105

**BOTSWANA**

CJ

Vorstershoop   26°00'S

38

Maleshe

Tshabong

25

Saron

McCarthy's Rest

38   33

49

CK

R380

Copyright © Map Studio 2005

22°00'E   23°00'E

Black Rock

63   64   65   66

29   30

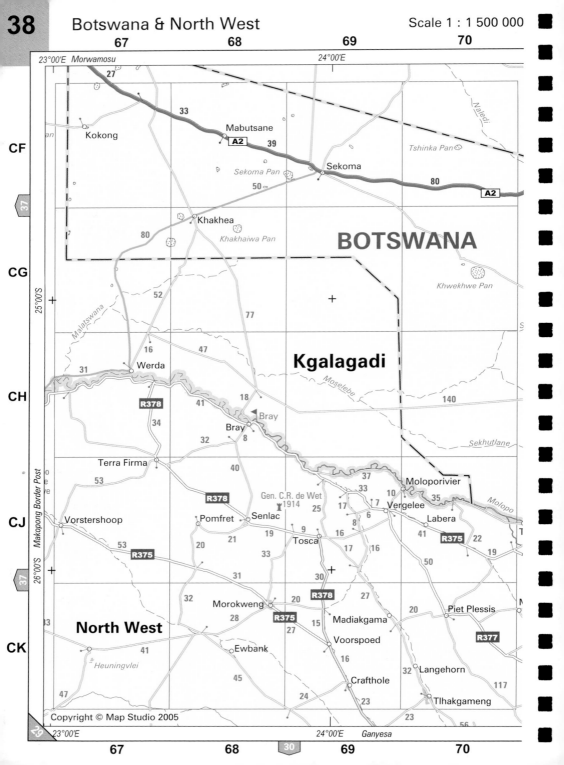

Copyright © Map Studio 2005

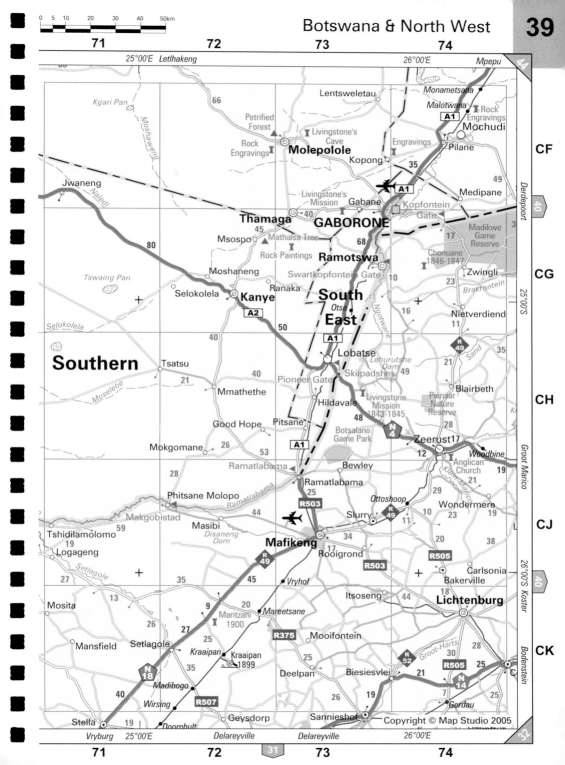

Copyright © Map Studio 2005

75    76    44    77    78

Kgatlong

27°00'E

Rooibosbult    Normandsdoring    Elmeston

Rooibokkraal    26

Sentrum    R510    Matlabas    57

*Waterberg*

60    55    Marakele National Park

**Limpopo**

CF

Silent Valley    17    18    Rankin's Pass

Sikwane    28    12    Oostermoed    33    18    Thabazimbi

Derdepoort    16    16    Ben Alberts Nature Reserve

35    15    Dwaalboom    21    15    ▲1345m    30    43

Kaya se put    31    Ganskuil    *Middelwit*    Tussenin    35    17    Rooiberg    23

CG    *Molatedi Dam*    Dwarsberg    *Biersprint*    *Bier*    39    Koedoeskop    14    Leeupoort    R516    26

25°00'S    Northam    22    22

Silkaatskop    +    33    Klipvoor Dam

Silkaatskop Monument    R510    15    Assen

35    Mabeskraal    *Mogwase*    Borakalalo Game Reserve

Straatsdrif    Pilanesberg Game Reserve    Motshikiri    R511    *Atlanta*

CH    Mabalstad    Sun City /    22    25    Beestekraal

Skuinsdrif    Lost City    *Vaalkop Dam*    36    SEE PAGES 56 - 57

*Kromellenboog Dam*    Lindleyspoort    R565    *Paul*    24    53    *Rooikoppies Dam*    Pansdrif

Riekertsdam    14    Boshoek    Bethanie

31    Marico Bosveld N. R.    Rusverby    26    Ga-Luka    *Bospoort Dam*    R556    Sonop    **Brits**

Groot Marico    Boekenhoutfontein 1873    R510    Bleskop    Maroelakop    De Wildt

19    24    7    Swartruggens    35    N4    Millvale    Mankano    Hartbeespoort    R513

Swartruggens    22    **Rustenburg**    19    Marikana    *Hartbeespoort Dam*    Kosmos    N4

27    *Twinbrook*    29    Magaliesberg Nature Area    T    48    Skeerpoort    R560

CJ    Lead Mine    29    29    Koster    24    *Olifantsnek Dam*    R24    Hekpoort    Cradle of Humankind (World Heritage Site)    52

R52    *Dessing*    Derby    Heldina    Maanhaarrand    R563

Grootpan    17    34    17    14    *Boons*    Magaliesburg    R24    **Randburg**

50    R52    Boons    53    **Krugersdorp**

44    10    R500    N14    **Roodepoort**

Swartplaas    36    49    **Randfontein**    **JOHANNESE**

**North West**    R30    Klerkskraal    14    R500    **Westonaria**    **Soweto**

Ga-Ramodingwana    37    *Bank*    35    Lenasia

Bodenstein    53    Ventersdorp    *Welverdiend*    11    Grasmere

Coligny    *Makokskraal*    Dovesdale    15    R28    Walkerville

50    Mesa    55    R501    Fochville    R82

Copyright © Map Studio 2005    *Dante Theron Monument*    **Sebokeng**

31    *Biesiesvlei*    27°00'E    Potchefstroom    Parys    Sebokeng

32

75    76    77    78

Copyright © Map Studio 2005

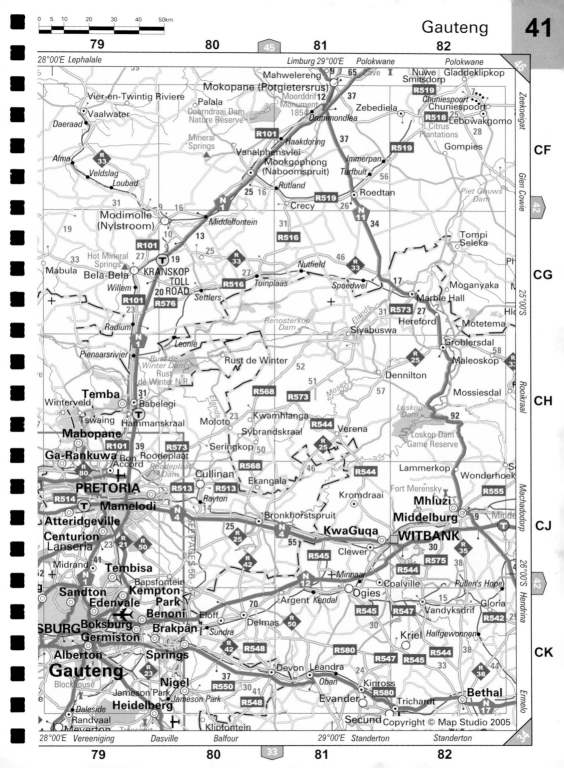

Copyright © Map Studio 2005

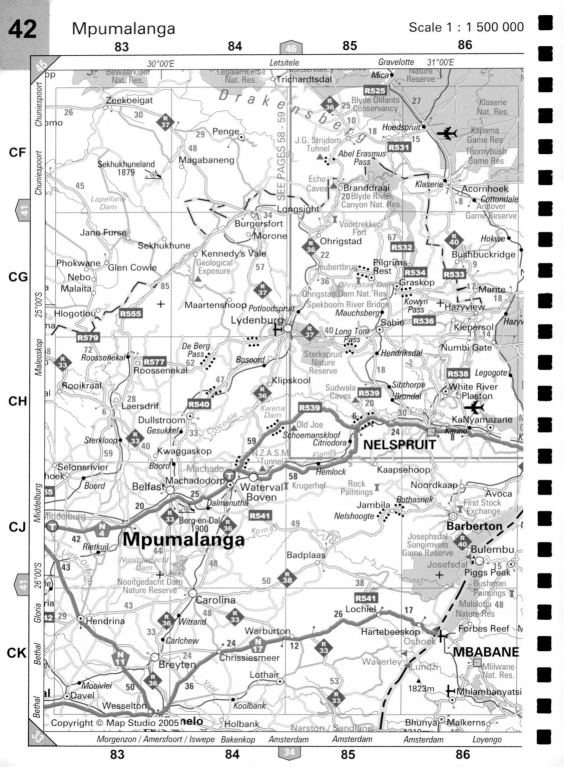

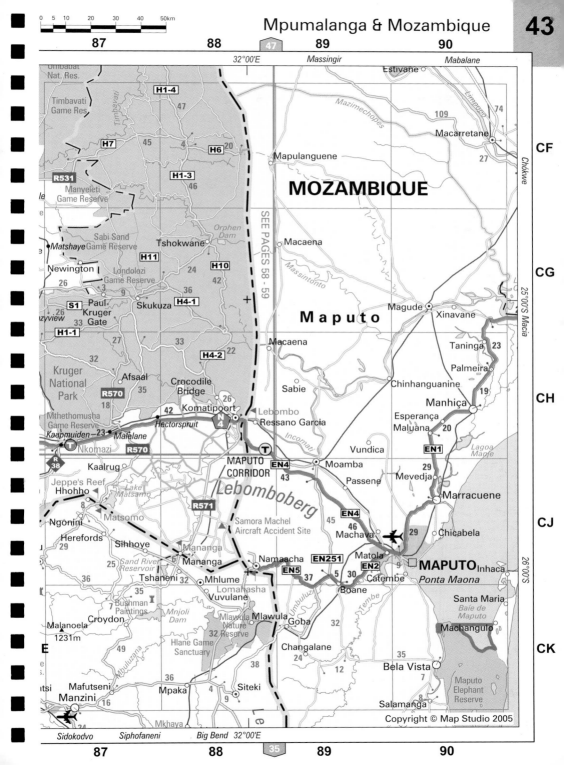

Copyright © Map Studio 2005

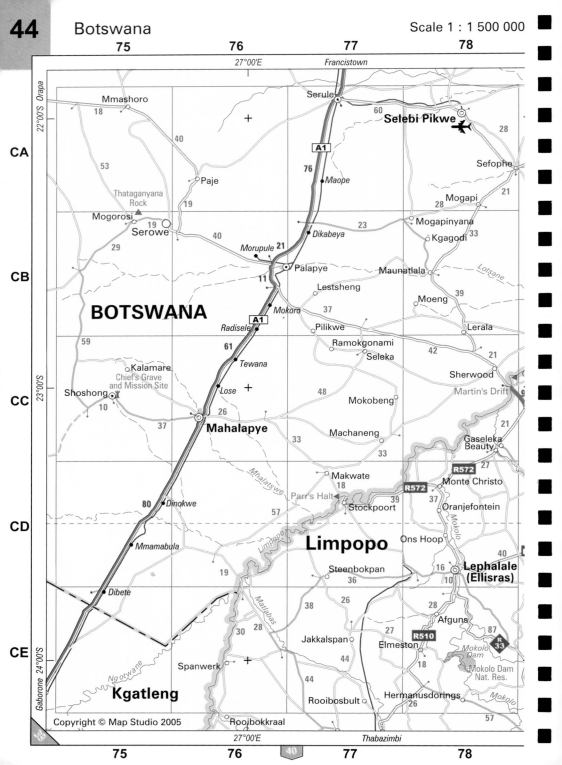

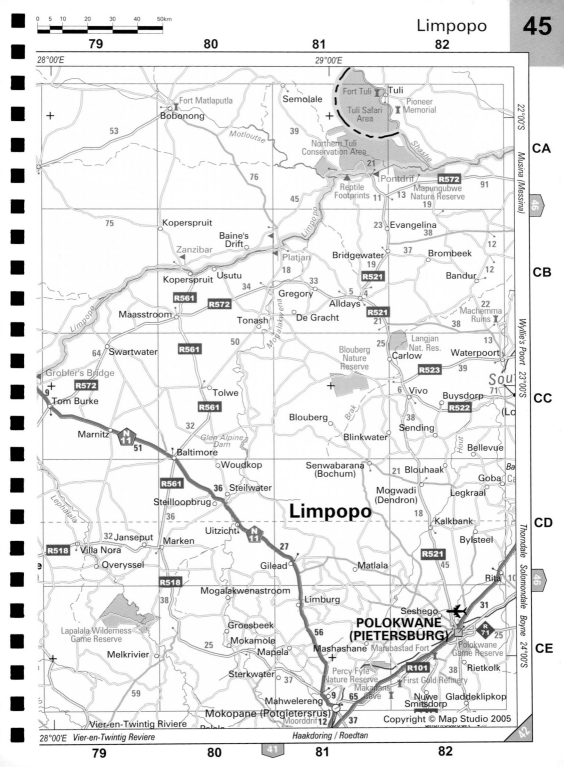

Copyright © Map Studio 2005

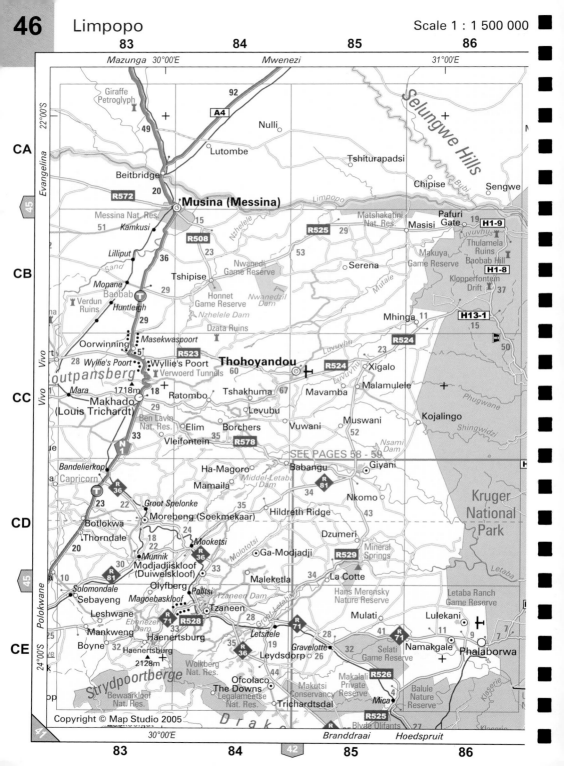

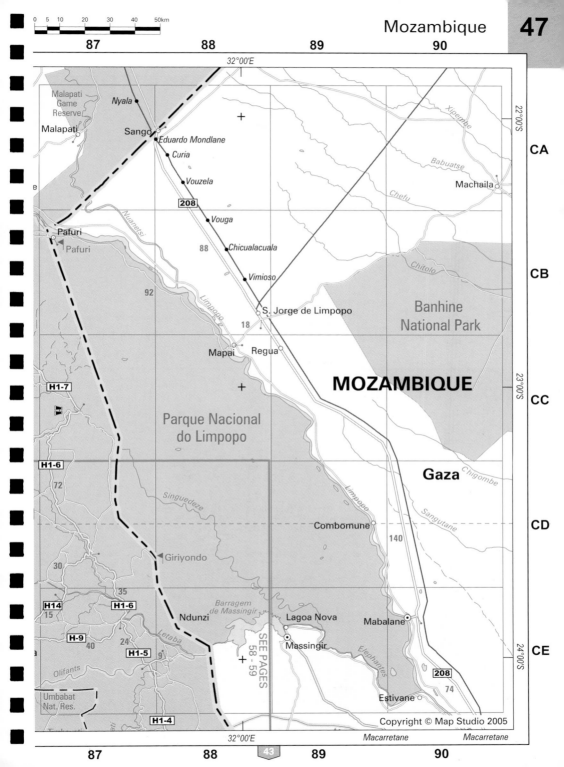

0 5 10    20    30    40    50km

87    88    89    90

*32°00'E*

Malapati
Game
Reserve
*Nyala*
Malapati
Sango
*Eduardo Mondlane*
*Curia*
*Vouzela*
**208**
*Vouga*
88    *Chicualacuala*
92    *Vimioso*
*Nuanetsi*
Pafuri
*Pafuri*
*Limpopo*
S. Jorge de Limpopo
18
Mapai    Regua

*Xipembe*

**CA**

*Babuatse*

*Chefu*    Machaila

*Chitolo*    **CB**

Banhine
National Park

**MOZAMBIQUE**

22°00'S

23°00'S

**H1-7**

Parque Nacional
do Limpopo

**Gaza**    *Chigombe*

**CC**

**H1-6**
72
*Singuedeze*
*Limpopo*
*Sangutane*

Combomune
140

**CD**

30
Giriyondo
*Letaba*

**H14**
15    **H1-6**
35
Ndunzi
*Barragem
de Massingir*
Lagoa Nova
Mabalane

**H-9**
40    24
**H1-5**    9
Massingir
*Elephantes*
*Olifants*

SEE PAGES
58 - 59

**208**
74

Umbabat
Nat. Res.

Estivane

**H1-4**

24°00'S

**CE**

Copyright © Map Studio 2005

*32°00'E*

43

*Macarretane*    *Macarretane*

87    88    89    90

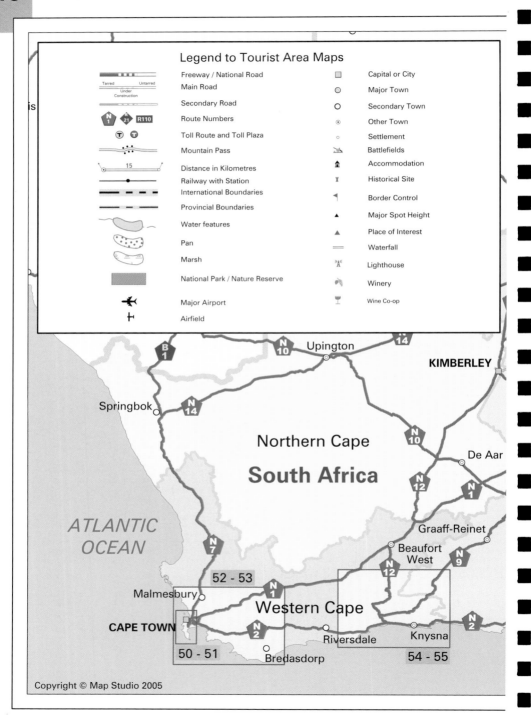

## Legend to Tourist Area Maps

| | |
|---|---|
| Freeway / National Road | ▫ Capital or City |
| Main Road | ◎ Major Town |
| Secondary Road | ○ Secondary Town |
| Route Numbers | ⊙ Other Town |
| Toll Route and Toll Plaza | ° Settlement |
| Mountain Pass | ⚔ Battlefields |
| Distance in Kilometres | 🏛 Accommodation |
| Railway with Station | ⚑ Historical Site |
| International Boundaries | ⚑ Border Control |
| Provincial Boundaries | ▲ Major Spot Height |
| Water features | ▲ Place of Interest |
| Pan | ═ Waterfall |
| Marsh | Lighthouse |
| National Park / Nature Reserve | Winery |
| Major Airport | Wine Co-op |
| Airfield | |

Tarred  Untarred
Under Construction

N1  21  R110

15

**KIMBERLEY**

Upington

Springbok

**Northern Cape**

**South Africa**

De Aar

**ATLANTIC OCEAN**

Graaff-Reinet

Beaufort West

52 - 53

Malmesbury

**Western Cape**

Riversdale

Knysna

**CAPE TOWN**

50 - 51

Bredasdorp

54 - 55

Copyright © Map Studio 2005

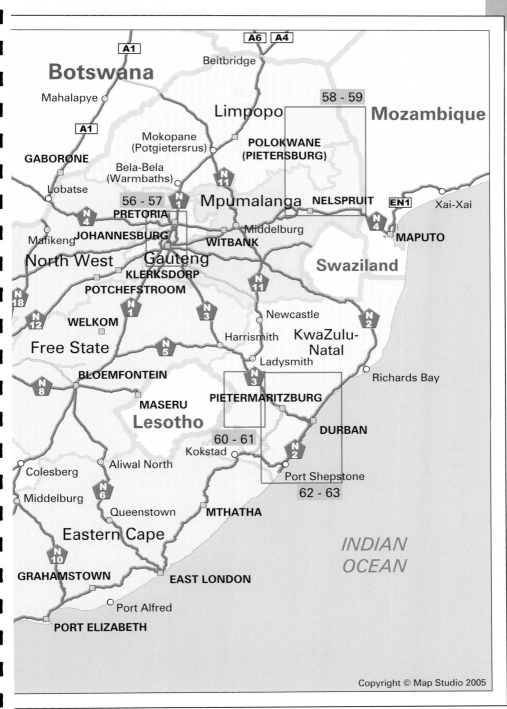

Copyright © Map Studio 2005

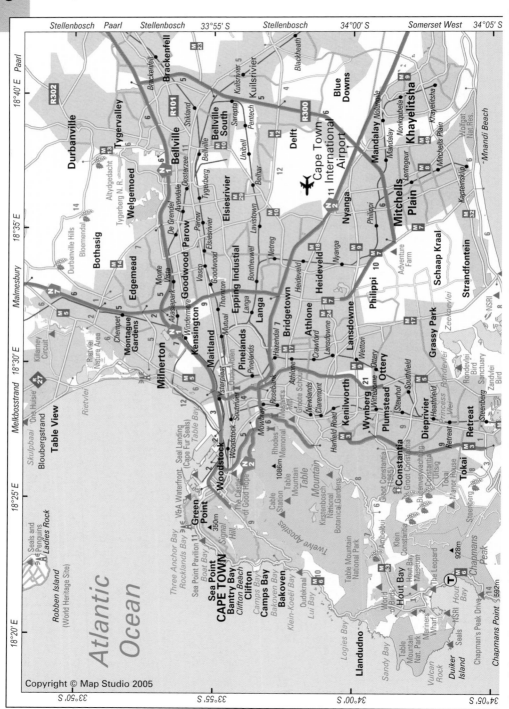

Copyright © Map Studio 2005

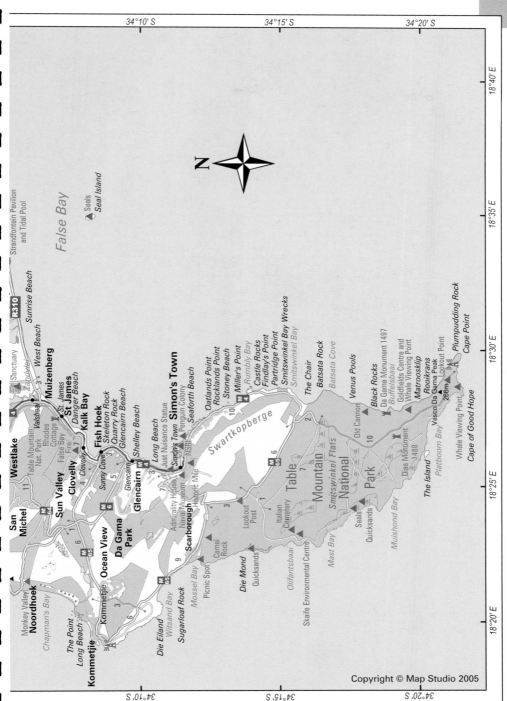

0    2.5    5    7.5    10km

N

False Bay

Seals
Seal Island

Strandfontein Pavilion
and Tidal Pool

R310

Sanctuary

Zandvlei

West Beach

Sunrise Beach

Muizenberg

Valsbaai

St. James
Danger Beach
Rhodes
Cottage

Kalk Bay

False Bay

St. James

Fish Hoek
Skeleton Rock
Quarry Rock
Glencairn Beach

Simon's Town

Simon's Town
Penguin Colony

Shelley Beach

Long Beach
Just Nuisance Statue
Seaforth Beach

Oatlands Point
Rocklands Point
Stoney Beach

Miller's Point

Rumbly Bay
Castle Rocks
Findlay's Point
Partridge Point

Smitswinkel Bay Wrecks
Smitswinkel Bay

The Chair
Batsata Rock
Batsata Cove

Venus Pools

Black Rocks
Da Gama Monument 1497
Buffelsbaai

Goldfields Centre and
Whale Viewing Point

Matroosklip
Rooikrans

Lookout Point

Plumpudding Rock
Cape Point

Old Cannon

Dias Monument

The Island
Platboom Bay
Vasco Da Gama Peak

Whale Viewing Point
Cape of Good Hope

266m

Swartkopberge

Table

Mountain

National

Park

Smitswinkel Flats

Italian
Cemetery

Seals
Quicksands

Muishond Bay

Mast Bay

Olifantsbaai

Skaife Environmental Centre

Lookout
Post

Westlake

San
Michel

Table Mountain
Nat. Park

Sun Valley

Clovelly

Glencairn

Da Gama
Park

Sunny Cove

Admiralty House
Naval Museum
Historic Mile

NSRI

Ocean View

Scarborough

Camel
Rock

Die Mond
Quicksands

Picnic Spot

Mossel Bay

Sugarloaf Rock

Die Eiland

Witsand Bay

Monkey Valley
Noordhoek

Chapman's Bay

The Point
Long Beach

Kommetjie

Copyright © Map Studio 2005

34°10' S    34°15' S    34°20' S

18°40' E    18°35' E    18°30' E    18°25' E    18°20' E

34°10' S    34°15' S    34°20' S

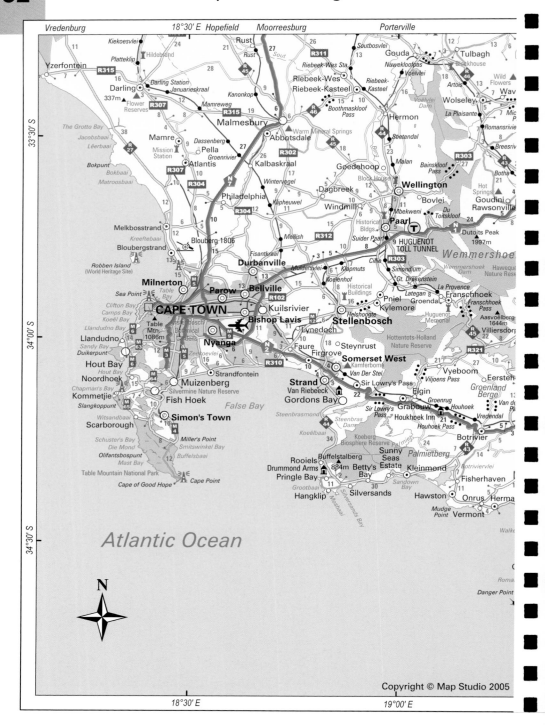

Copyright © Map Studio 2005

Copyright © Map Studio 2005

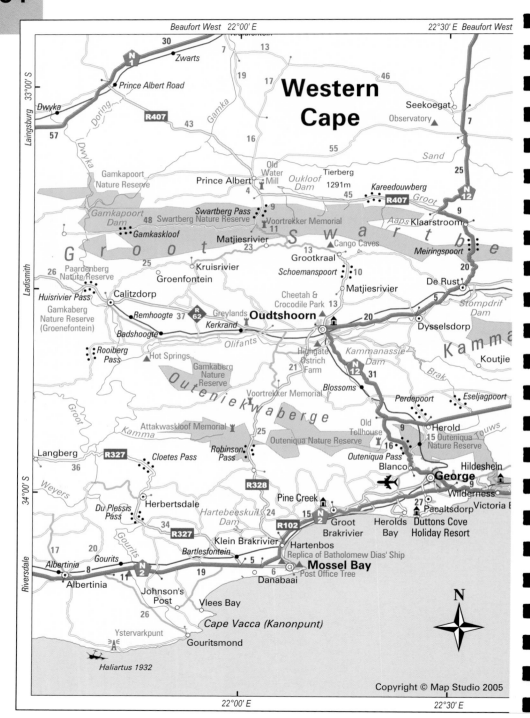

Copyright © Map Studio 2005

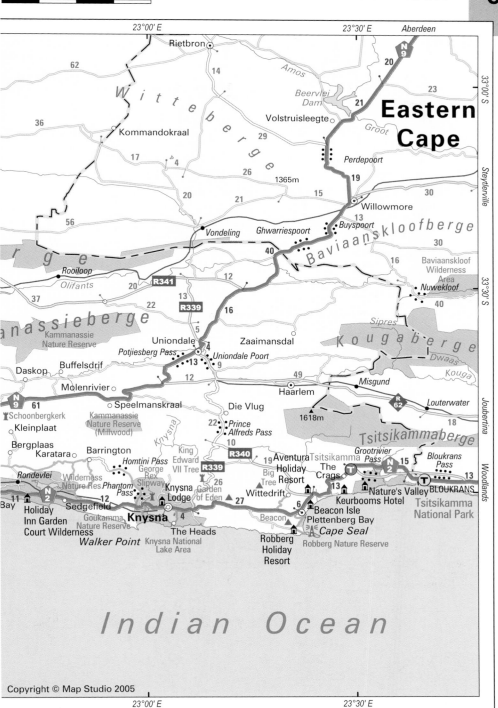

0 10 20 30 40km

23°00' E       23°30' E    Aberdeen

Rietbron

N9

62    14    20

*Amos*

*Beervlei Dam*    21    23

33°00' S

Volstruisleegte

36    Kommandokraal    29    **Eastern Cape**

*Groot*

17    4    26    Perdepoort

1365m    19

*W i t t e b e r g e*

20    21    15    30

Steytlerville

56    Vondeling    Ghwarriespoort    Buyspoort    13    Willowmore

*B a v i a a n s k l o o f b e r g e*

40    30

*r g e*    Rooiloop    16    Baviaanskloof Wilderness Area

33°30' S

*Olifants*    12    R341    Nuwekloof

37    20    22    13    16    40

*n a s s i e b e r g e*    R339

*Sipres*

Kammanassie Nature Reserve    5    *K o u g a b e r g e*

Uniondale    4    Zaaimansdal

*Dwaas*

Potjiesberg Pass    13    Uniondale Poort    9    *Kouga*

Daskop    Buffelsdrif    12    49    Misgund    Louterwater

Molenrivier    Haarlem

N9    61    Speelmanskraal    Die Vlug    1618m    R62    18

Schoonbergkerk

Kleinplaat    Kammanassie Nature Reserve (Millwood)    22    Prince Alfreds Pass    *T s i t s i k a m m a b e r g e*

Bergplaas    Karatara    Barrington    10    *Grootrivier Pass*    15    Bloukrans Pass

Homtini Pass    King Edward VII Tree    R340    19    Aventura Holiday Resort    Tsitsikamma    N2    BLOUKRANS    13

Joubertina

Woodlands

*Rondevlei*    George    R339    Big Tree    The Crags    13    Nature's Valley

Wilderness Nature Res    Phantom Pass    Rex Slipway    Garden of Eden    26    Wittedrift    Keurbooms Hotel    Tsitsikamma National Park

Bay    11    N2    12    Knysna Lodge    27    6    Beacon Isle Plettenberg Bay

Holiday Inn Garden Court Wilderness    Sedgefield    Goukamma Nature Reserve    **Knysna**    4    Beacon    *Cape Seal*

*Walker Point*    The Heads    Knysna National Lake Area    Robberg Holiday Resort    Robberg Nature Reserve

*I n d i a n   O c e a n*

Copyright © Map Studio 2005

23°00' E        23°30' E

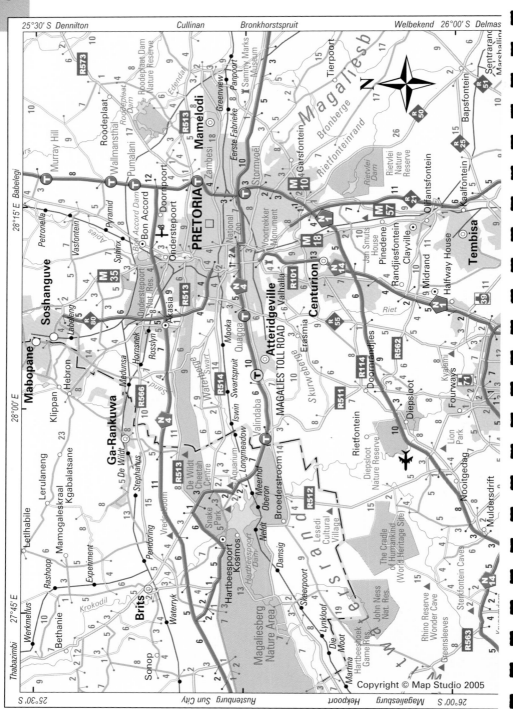

Copyright © Map Studio 2005

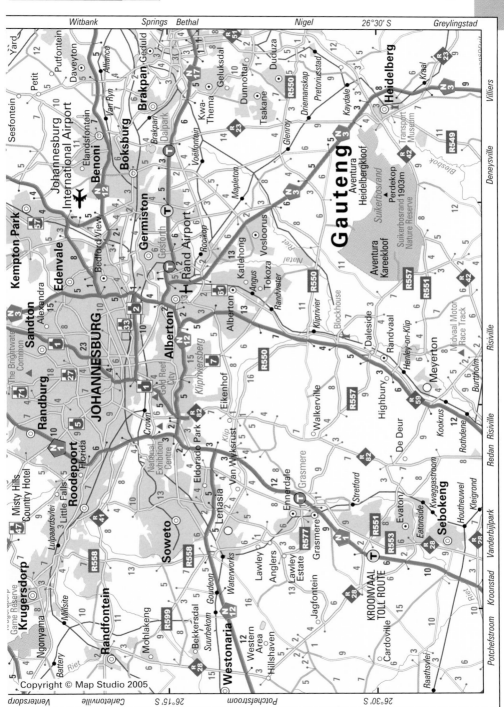

Copyright © Map Studio 2005

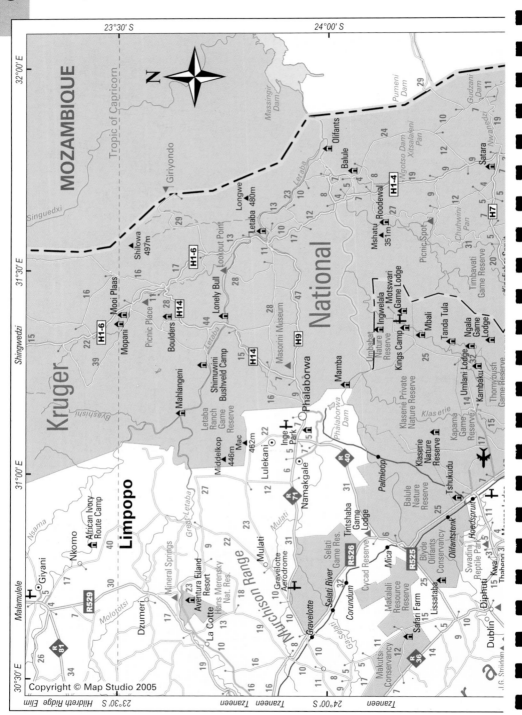

Copyright © Map Studio 2005

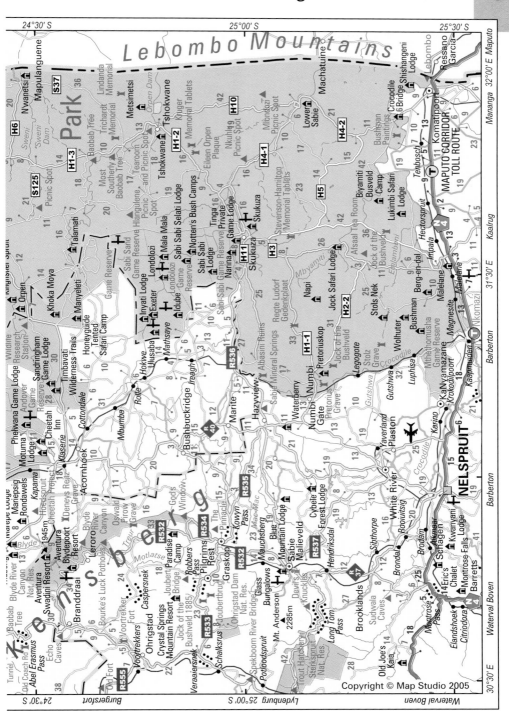

Copyright © Map Studio 2005

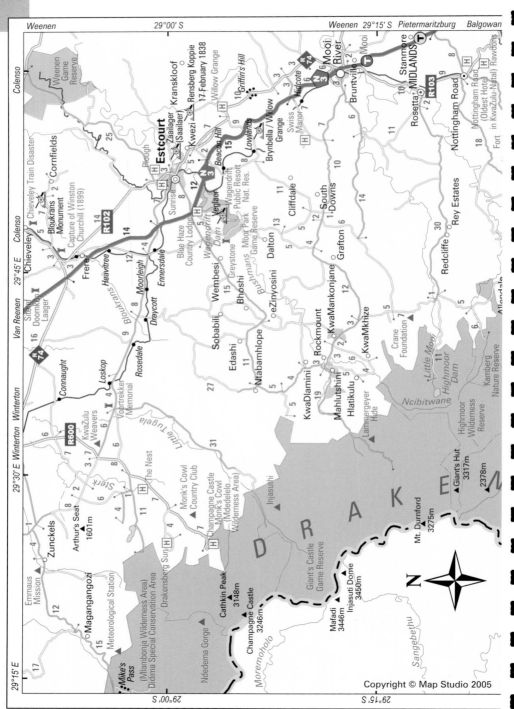

Copyright © Map Studio 2005

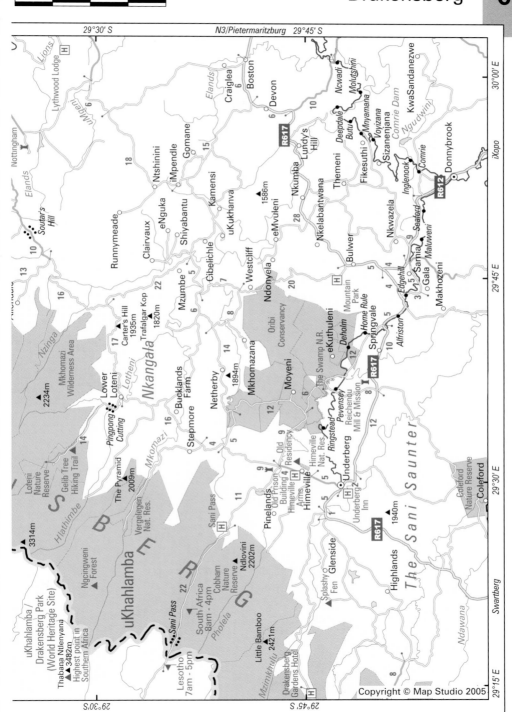

0  5  10  15  20km

29°30' S    N3/Pietermaritzburg    29°45' S

Lythwood Lodge
Nottingham
Soutar's Hill
Lions
uMgeni
Elands

Craiglea
Boston
Devon
Elands
Ncwadi
Molutshini
Deepdale
Butu
Mnyamana
Voyizana
Sizanenjana
KwaSandanezwe
Comrie Dam
Ngudwini
iXopo

R617
Lundy's Hill
Themeni
Fikesuthi
Inglenook
Comrie
Seaford
Donnybrook
R612

Gomane
Ntshinini
iMpendle
Kamensi
uKukhanva
Nkumba
Nkelabantwana
Nkwazela
Samia
Gala
Maluweni
Makhozeni

Runnymeade
Clairvaux
eNguka
Shiyabantu
Cibelichle
Westcliff
eMvuleni
1586m
Bulwer
Edgehill
29°45' E

Nzinga
Mkhomazi Wilderness Area
Carter's Hill 1935m
Trafalgar Kop 1820m
Mzumbe
Netherby
1894m
Mkhomazana
Moyeni
Oribi Conservancy
Ndonyela
Mountain Park
eKuthuleni
Deholm
Home Rule
Springvale
Alfriston
The Swamp N.R.

2234m
Lower Loteni
Pingpong Cutting
Nkangala
Loteni
Bucklands Farm
Stepmore
Mkomazi
Pevensey
Reichenau Mill & Mission
Ringstead
Underberg
Himeville Nat. Res.

Loteni Nature Reserve
Gelib Tree Hiking Trail
The Pyramid 2009m
Vergelegen Nat. Res.
Hlathimbe
Old Prison
Old Building 4 Residency
Himeville
Himeville Arms
Underberg Inn
1940m
R617

3334m
Ngcingweni Forest
Sani Pass
Pinelands
Highlands
Glenside
Splashy Fen
Coleford
Coleford Nature Reserve

uKhahlamba / Drakensberg Park (World Heritage Site)
Thabana Ntlenyana 3482m
Highest point in Southern Africa
uKhahlamba
Lesotho 7am - 5pm
Sani Pass
South Africa 8am - 4pm
Cobham Nature Reserve
Ndlovini 2202m
Little Bamboo 2421m
Pholela
Mzimkhulu
Drakensberg Gardens Hotel

The Sani Saunter
Swartberg
Ndawana

Copyright © Map Studio 2005

29°30'S    29°45'S    29°15' E

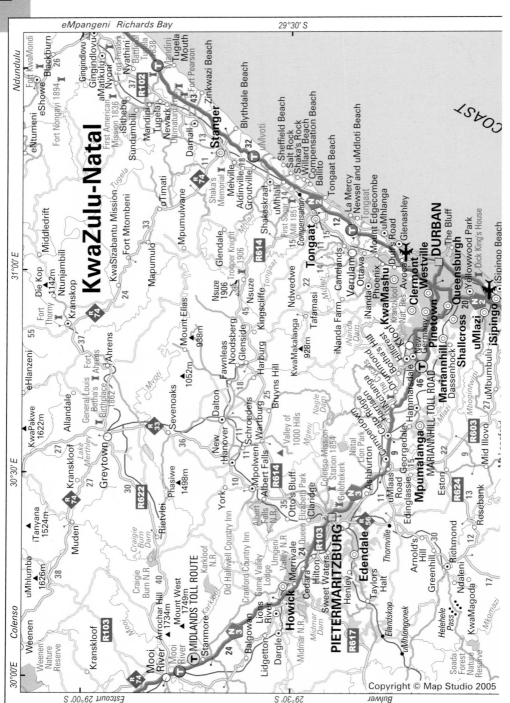

eMpangeni  Richards Bay

29°30' S

COAST

Ndundulu

KwaZulu-Natal

31°00' E

30°30' E

30°00'E

Colenso

Estcourt 29°00'S

S °00'S 29

29°30'S

Bulwer

Fort KwaMondi
eShowe
Blackburn 26
eNtumeni
Gingindlovu
Gingindlovu
aMatikulu
Nyoni
Fort Trealort
Nyathini
1838
Fort Nongayi 1894
eHlanzeni
First American
Mission 1836
iSithebe
Mandini
Newark
Tugela
Tugela Mouth
Battle
R102
37
R102
43 Fort Pearson
Zinkwazi Beach

Sundumbili
Mpumulwane
Darnall
11
Stanger
Blythdale Beach

KwaSizabantu Mission
Fort Mtombeni
Timati
13
uMvoti
Sheffield Beach

KwaZulu-Natal

Middledrift
Ntunjambili
Die Kop
1142m
Thorny
Fort
Kranskop
Mpumulo
33
Shaka's
Memorial
Melville
Aldinville
18
Groutville
Shakaskraal
R614
uMhlali
Salt Rock
Shaka's Rock
Willard Beach
Compensation Beach
Ballito
Tongaat Beach

55
Fort
eHlanzeni
Ahrens
R74
Kranskop
24
Mapumulo
Mount Elias
938m
Nsuze
1906
Nsuze
Kingscliffe
45
Trooper Knight
T 1906
uMhlali
First Sugar 14
Mill 1851
15
Compensation
N
2
La Mercy
Newsel and uMdloti Beach
Mount Edgecombe
uMhlanga
Glenashley

General Louis
Botha's
Birthplace
1862
KwaPakwe
1622m
Allandale
Sevenoaks
Fawnleas
Noodsberg
Glenside
1052m
Harburg
Bruyns Hill
Tafamasi
928m
12
Tongaat
Canelands
Verulam
Ottawa
iNanda
Phoenix
KwaMashu
Nat. Res. Avoca
Duff's Road
DURBAN
Westville
The Bluff
Yellowwood Park
Dick King's House

iTanyana
1524m
Krankskloof
27
Greytown
R74
30
R622
Phasiwe
1498m
New Hanover
11
Schroeders
Mpolweni
Wartburg
25
Nagle
Dam
KwaMakalanga
iNanda Farm
iNanda
Dam
Hillcrest
New Germany
Pinetown
Marianhill
Dassenhock
Shallcross
uMlazi
iSipingo
Sipingo Beach

Muden
Rietvlei
R74
York
10
Albert Falls
R614
Otto's Bluff
Valley of
1000 Hills
Mgeni
Drummond
Botha's Hill
Bothas
Kloof
Krantzkloof
Assagay
Hammarsdale
MARIANHILL TOLL ROAD
46
Mariannhill
Georgedale
Mpumalanga
R603

uMhlumba
1626m
38
Craigie
Burn
Dam
Stanmore
Midmar
Dam
Albert
Falls
N.R
Colenso Mission
Station 1854
Geelhekerk
Claridge
Cedara
Merrivale
Hilton
Sweet Waters
PIETERMARITZBURG
Edendale
R103
56
Ashburton
Natal
Lion Park
Caterdown
uMlaas
Road
Thornville
Edinglassie
Eston
Georgedale
15
9
9
R624
13
Rosebank
Mid Illovo
R603

KwaPakwe
Kranskloof
Weenen
Weenen
Nature
Reserve
R103
Mooi
River
Mooi
River
T
R74
24
MIDLANDS TOLL ROUTE
N
3
Lidgetton
Dargle
Balgowan
Lions
River
Midmar N.R.
Arrochar Hill 1734m
Mount West
1749m
Craigie
Burn N.R
40
Karkloof
Cranford Country Inn
Old Halliwell Country Inn
Albert
Falls
Valley N.R
Umgeni
Valley N.R
Henley
Taylors
Halt
Elandskop
uMhlongonek
Helehele
Pass
KwaMagoda
Mkomazi
Arnold's
Hill
Greenhill
Richmond
Ndaleni
12
30
17
Soada
Forest
Nature
Reserve

R617

Copyright © Map Studio 2005

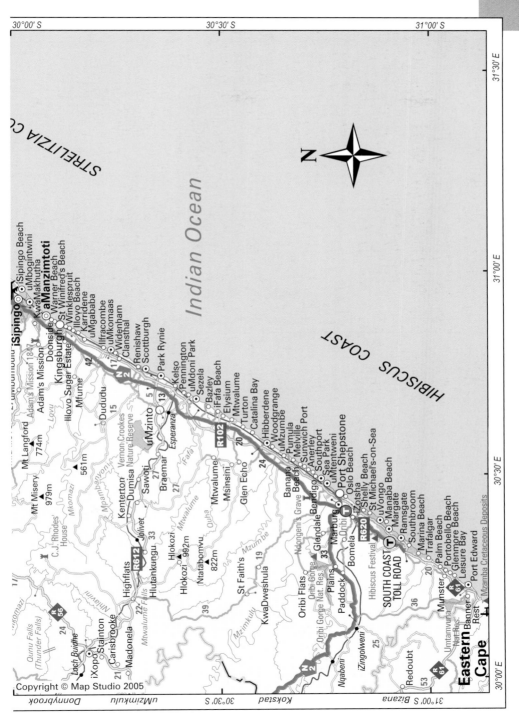

Copyright © Map Studio 2005

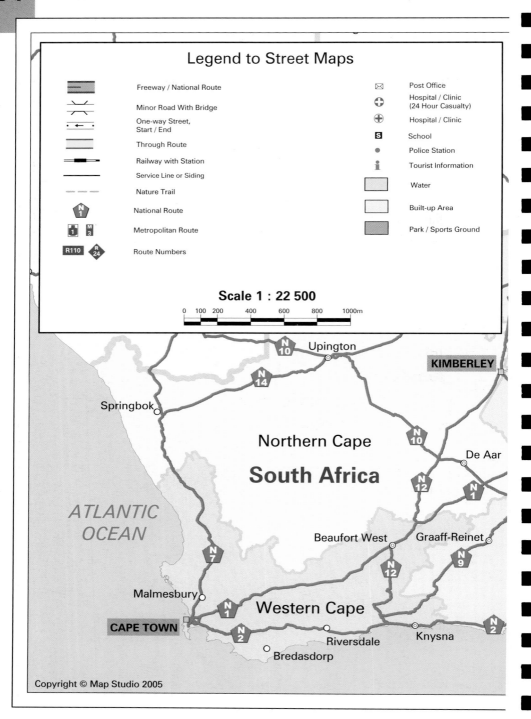

## Legend to Street Maps

| | |
|---|---|
| Freeway / National Route | ⊠ Post Office |
| Minor Road With Bridge | ⊕ Hospital / Clinic (24 Hour Casualty) |
| One-way Street, Start / End | ⊕ Hospital / Clinic |
| Through Route | **S** School |
| Railway with Station | • Police Station |
| Service Line or Siding | **i** Tourist Information |
| Nature Trail | Water |
| National Route | Built-up Area |
| Metropolitan Route | Park / Sports Ground |
| R110 / 24 Route Numbers | |

### Scale 1 : 22 500

0   100   200    400    600    800    1000m

Upington

**KIMBERLEY**

Springbok

Northern Cape

**South Africa**

De Aar

*ATLANTIC OCEAN*

N12

N1

Beaufort West

Graaff-Reinet

N9

Malmesbury

N12

N7

N1

**CAPE TOWN**

Western Cape

N2

Knysna

N2

Riversdale

Bredasdorp

Copyright © Map Studio 2005

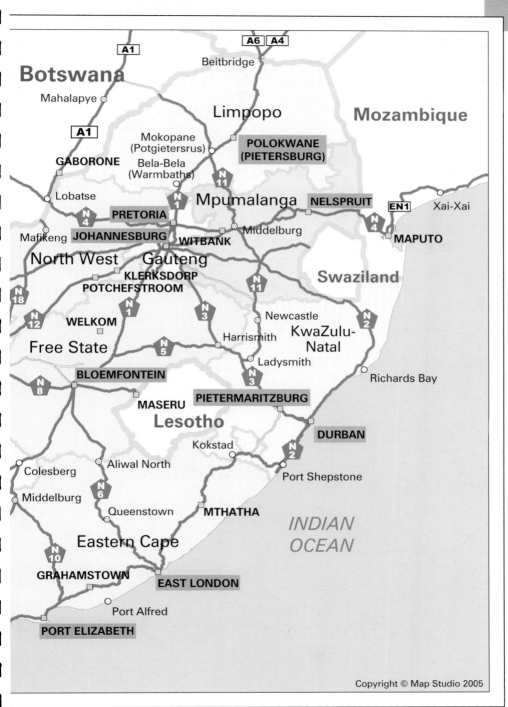

Copyright © Map Studio 2005

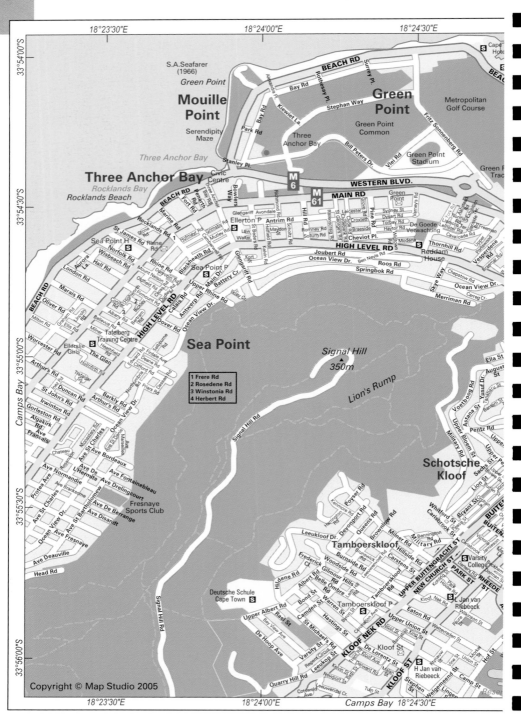

Copyright © Map Studio 2005

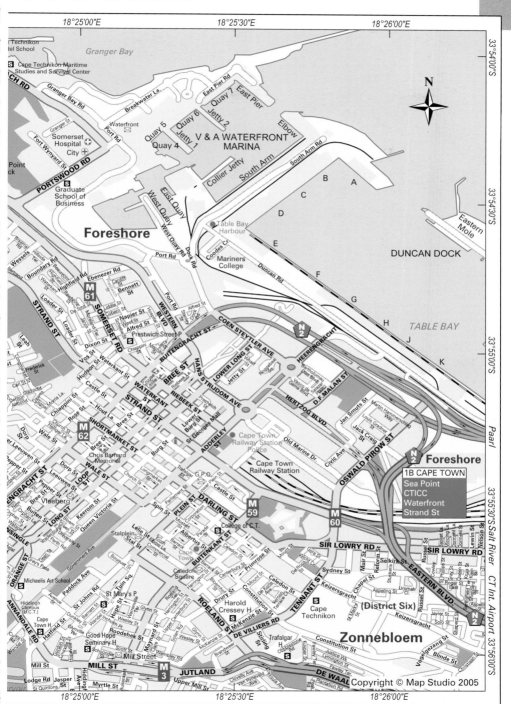

0    500    1 000m

18°25'00"E    18°25'30"E    18°26'00"E

33°54'00"S
33°54'30"S
33°55'00"S
33°55'30"S
33°56'00"S

N

Technikon Hotel School
Cape Technikon Maritime Studies and Survival Center
Granger Bay

Granger Bay Rd
Breakwater La.
East Pier Rd
Quay 7  East Pier
Jetty 2
Quay 6  Elbow
Quay 5  Jetty 1
Waterfront
Port Rd
Granger Granville
Somerset Hospital City
Fort Wynard
Quay 4
V & A WATERFRONT MARINA
Collier Jetty
South Arm
South Arm Rd

PORTSWOOD RD
Graduate School of Business

West Quay Rd
West Quay Rd
Dock Rd
Port Rd
Table Bay Harbour
Coodes Crt
Mariners College
Duncan Rd

Foreshore

B  A
C
D
E
F
G
H
J
K

DUNCAN DOCK

Eastern Mole

TABLE BAY

STRAND ST
SOMERSET RD

M 61

WESTERN BLVD
COEN STEYTLER AVE
HEERENGRACHT
HERTZOG BLVD
D.F. MALAN ST
OSWALD PIROW ST

N2

Foreshore

1B CAPE TOWN
Sea Point
CTICC
Waterfront
Strand St

BUITENGRACHT ST
BREE ST
HANS STRIJDOM AVE
LOWER LONG ST
JETTY ST
Vasco da Gama Blvd
Jan Smuts St
Louis Gradner St
Martin Hammerschlag Way
Jack Craig St

WATERKANT ST
STRAND ST
RIEBEEK ST
Lower Burg St
St Georges Mall
ADDERLEY ST
Cape Town Railway Station Police
Old Marine Dr.
Civic Ave

SHORTMARKET ST
WALE ST
LOOP ST
DARLING ST
PLEIN ST
Cape Town Railway Station

M 62
M 59
M 60

Chris Barnard Memorial
Church St
G.P.O.
Castle St
College of C.T.

SIR LOWRY RD
SIR LOWRY RD
EASTERN BLVD

Sydney St
Muir St
Reform St
Selkirk St

BUITENKANT ST
Caledon St
Primrose St
Keizersgracht
Chapel St

(District Six)

ROELAND ST
TENNANT ST
DE VILLIERS RD
Cape Technikon
Keizersgracht

S

Zonnebloem

Michaelis Art School
St Mary's H
Harold Cressey H
Good Hope Seminary H

Constitution St
Trafalgar H

MILL ST
JUTLAND
DE WAAL

M 3

Upper Mill St

Copyright © Map Studio 2005

18°25'00"E    18°25'30"E    18°26'00"E

Grahamstown/East London   25°37'00"E      25°37'30"E      25°38'00"E

**PORT ELIZABETH**
Albany Rd Interchange
Albany Rd M7

Walmer

Humansdorp / N2   33°57'30"S

Diesel St
Herold St
Devon St
St Patricks Rd
GOVAN MBEKI AVE
Lespade St
Korsten St
Frederick
Callington St
St Stephens St
Tulla St
Richmond Hill St
R102
Dagbre
Teachers S
Centre
Evatt St
Smith
Phillip St
Irvine St
Landsdowne St
Claredon C
Meacham St
Clyde St
Stanley St
Moffat St
Edward St
Hunt St
Kemsley St
Cross St
Raleigh St
Campbell St
Dollery S
RUSSELL RD
Chapel La
Hill St
Victoria St
BAAKENS ST
Port
Elizabeth
Chapel St
Ivy St
Donkin
Hill
Court St
P.E College
R102
Centrahill S
Parliament St
Municipal St
Havelock
Sq.
Alfred Ter
Construction
DONKIN
RESERVE
Whites Rd
Castle Hill
RINK ST
Robson St
Clyde St
Lawrence St
Rosa St
Whitlock St
Prospect Hill
Military Rd
Cuyler Cr.
Central
Havelock St
Pearson St
Museum St
Trinity S
Bird St
Trader
Sq.
Belmont Ter.
Military Cr.
St Georges
Hospital
Western St
Drake St
Cuyler Cr.
Sutton
Annerley Ter
Twickenham
St
Fort St
VALLEY RD
St Georges
Park
Cuyler St
Gordon Ter.
Cuyler Cr.
Park Dr.
Forbes Ave
Jutland Cr.
BRICKMAKERS KLOOF
Gardner Cir.
Harris
Cr.
Cudmore
Bridge
Ellis St
M9
Hunter
Ave
S
Greenwood P
Chidmore
Pier St
HUMEWOOD RD
M4
SETTLERS PARK
NATURE RESERVE
Baakens
Upper Valley Rd
Seymour St
South
End
WALMER BLVD.
Lawhill Rd
Oakworth Rd
Outenia
1
Fordyce Rd
Pigott
La.
Frere Cr.
Sayre Cr.
Newcon Rd
Passat St
Wyndham St
Kinsley
Cr.
Mitchell St
Pamir St
Thekla
Chapman
1st Ave
Balfour St
Anderson
Humewood
Perrot
Ave
Cir.
Webber St
WALMER RD
Karmin
Dr.
Lea Pl.
Humerail Sports
Ground
M9
Partridge Ave
Butters
Ave
Hoy
Ave
Randell
Ave St
Emily St
Mitchell St
Duncan Ave
Lea Pl.
Victoria Park H
S
Victoria Park Dr.
Victoria Park
Old Boys'
Sports Ground
Forest Hill Rd
Albert Rd
1st Ave
Ernest Walter Ave
SOUTH END
CEMETERY
Humewood
2nd
Ave
VICTORIA
PARK
Elizabeth
Donkin
Woodhead Dr.
Hilton Cr
Union Rd
Victoria Park
Grey P
S
Valley
M11
LA ROCHE DR.
Hilton Cr
Lucerne Ave
Clover Cr.
Protea Dr.
Heather Sq.
Heather Sq.
33°59'00"S Walmer
ALLISTER MILLER DR.
Willow Dr.
Forest Rd
Hill Dr.
Tacoma Pl.
Aloe St
Orange Grove
Orange Grove
S
Pro

25°37'00"E      25°37'30"E      25°38'00"E

Copyright © Map Studio 2005

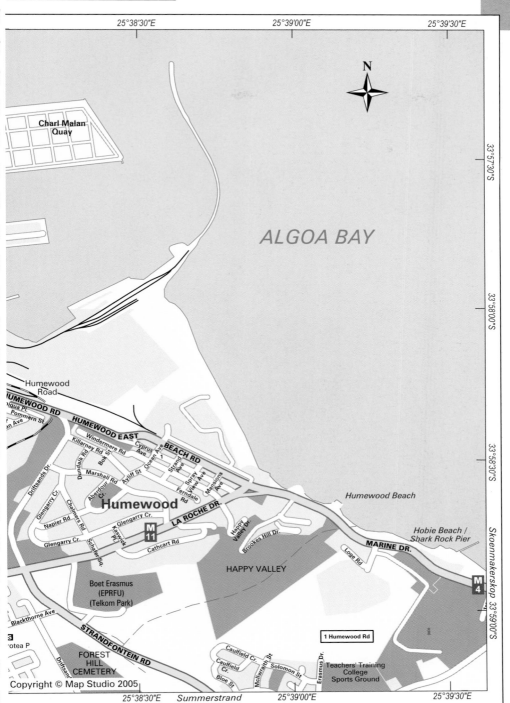

Copyright © Map Studio 2005

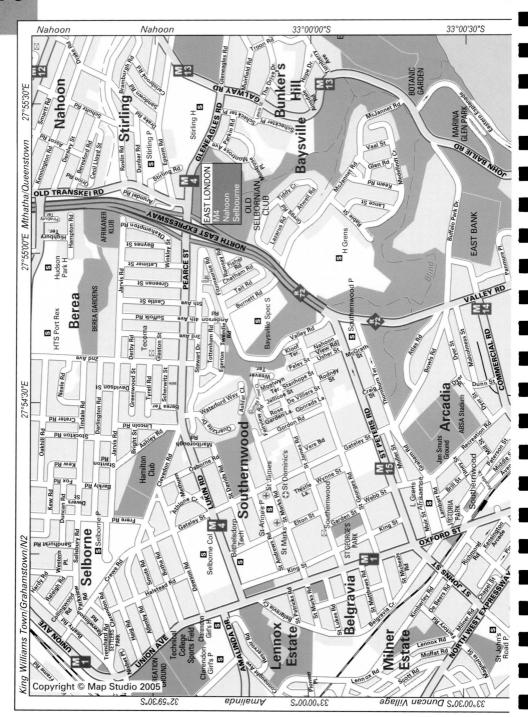

EAST LONDON
M4
Nahoon
Selbourne

Copyright © Map Studio 2005

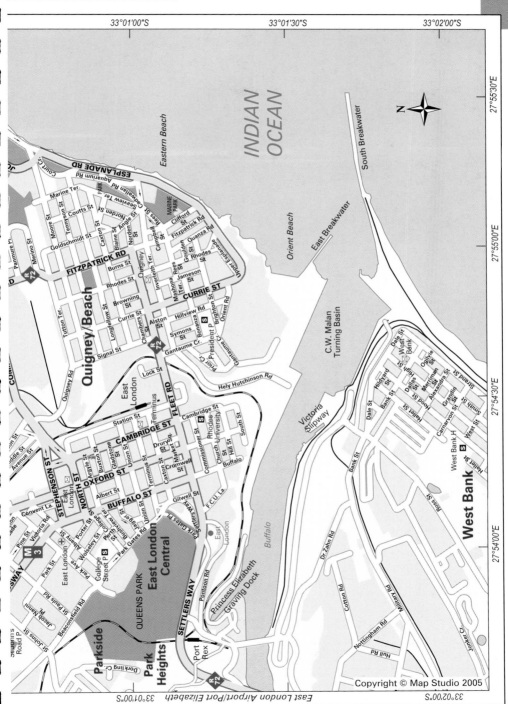

0 500 1 000m

33°01'00"S      33°01'30"S      33°02'00"S

INDIAN OCEAN

N

Eastern Beach

Orient Beach

East Breakwater

South Breakwater

27°55'30"E

27°55'00"E

27°54'30"E

27°54'00"E

MARINE PARK

ESPLANADE RD

FITZPATRICK RD

Quigney/Beach

CURRIE ST

CAMBRIDGE ST

NORTH OXFORD ST

BUFFALO ST

STEPHENSON ST

FLEET RD

East London

Station St

Terminus

East London Central

QUEENS PARK

Park Heights

Parkside

SETTLERS WAY

Port Rex

Princess Elizabeth Graving Dock

Buffalo

Victoria Slipway

C.W. Malan Turning Basin

West Bank

Hely Hutchinson Rd

M 3

Copyright © Map Studio 2005

33°01'00"S      East London Airport/Port Elizabeth      33°02'00"S

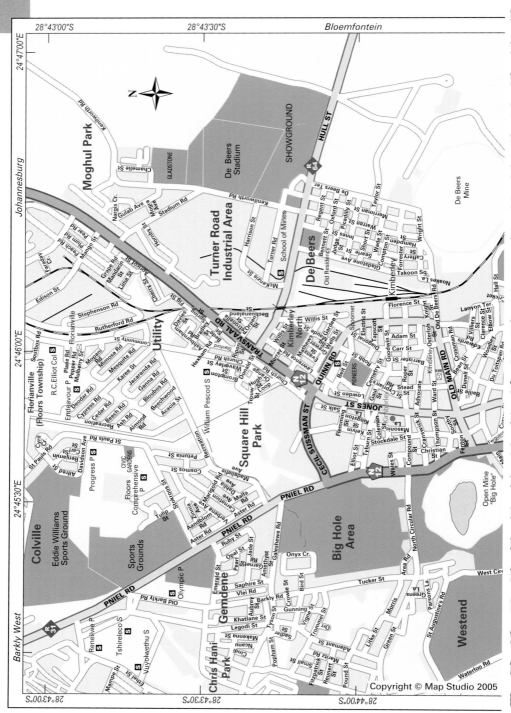

Copyright © Map Studio 2005

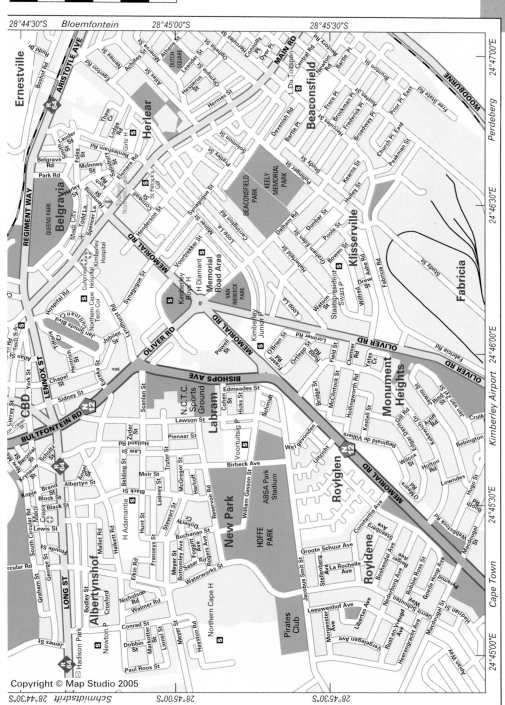

Copyright © Map Studio 2005

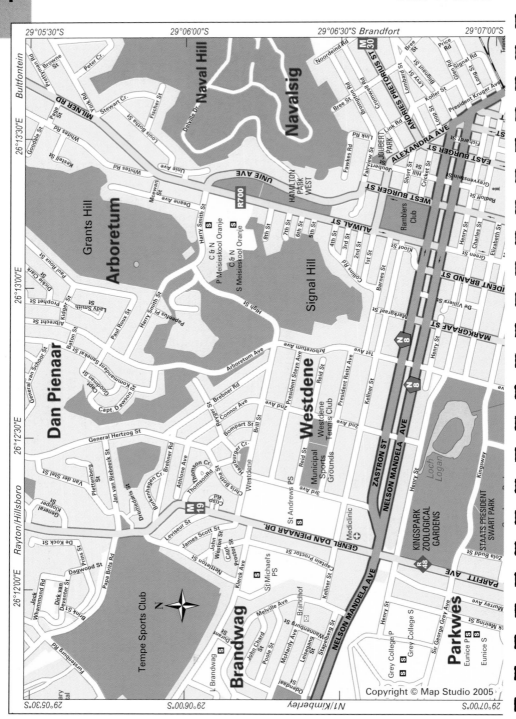

Copyright © Map Studio 2005

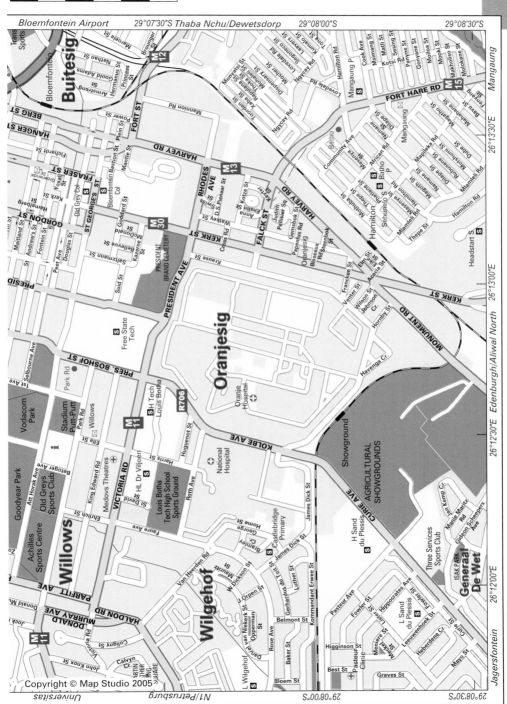

Copyright © Map Studio 2005

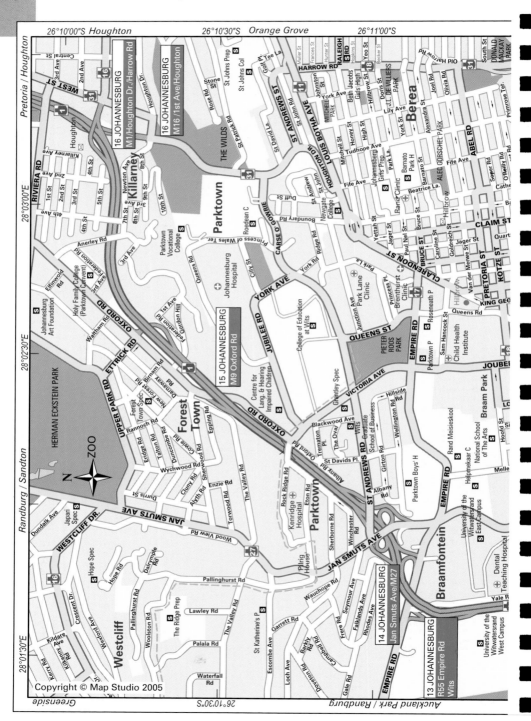

Copyright © Map Studio 2005

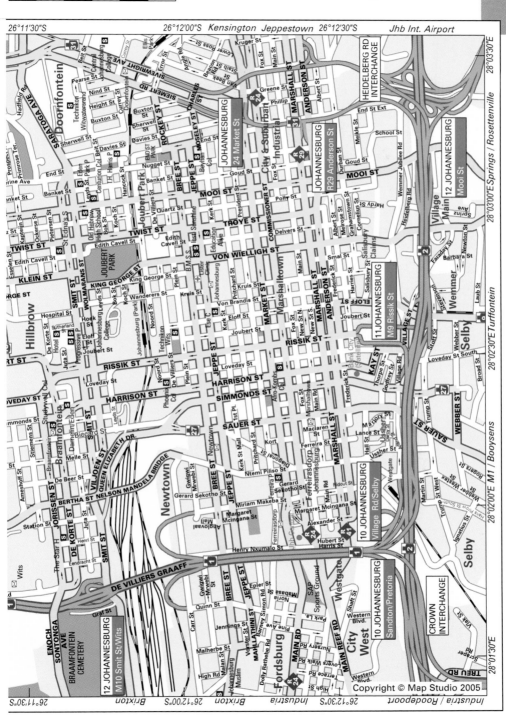

Copyright © Map Studio 2005

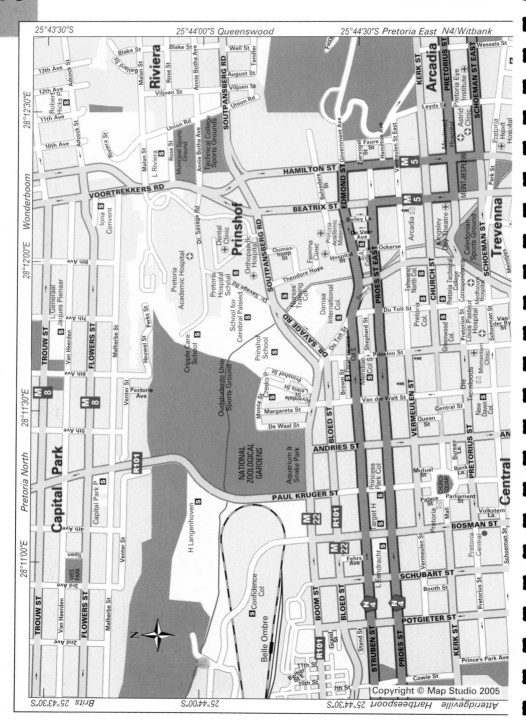

Copyright © Map Studio 2005

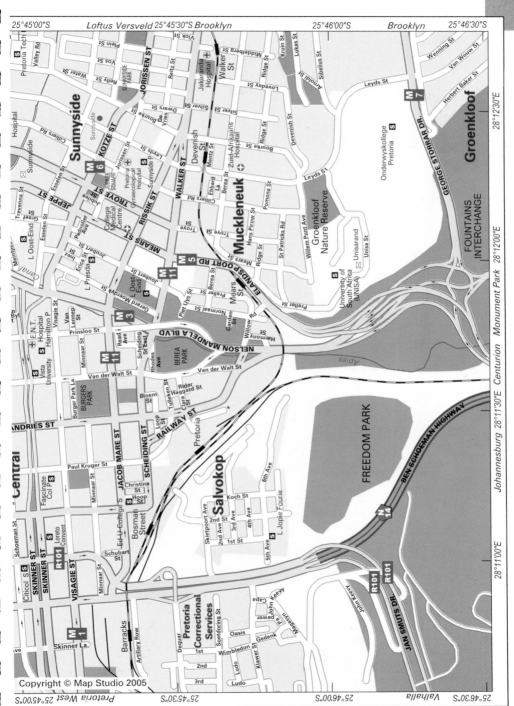

0 500 1 000m

25°45'00"S  Loftus Versveld  25°45'30"S Brooklyn  25°46'00"S  Brooklyn  25°46'30"S

Sunnyside

Muckleneuk

Groenkloof

Groenkloof Nature Reserve

University of South Africa (UNISA)

Onderwyskollege Pretoria

FOUNTAINS INTERCHANGE

Central

Salvokop

FREEDOM PARK

NELSON MANDELA BLVD

BEREA PARK

BURGERS PARK

Pretoria Correctional Services

JAN SMUTS DR.

BEN SCHOEMAN HIGHWAY

GEORGE STORRAR DR.

28°12'30"E

28°12'00"E

28°11'30"E

28°11'00"E

Johannesburg 28°11'30"E Centurion Monument Park 28°12'00"E

Pretoria West 25°45'00"S  25°45'30"S  25°46'00"S  Valhalla 25°46'30"S

Copyright © Map Studio 2005

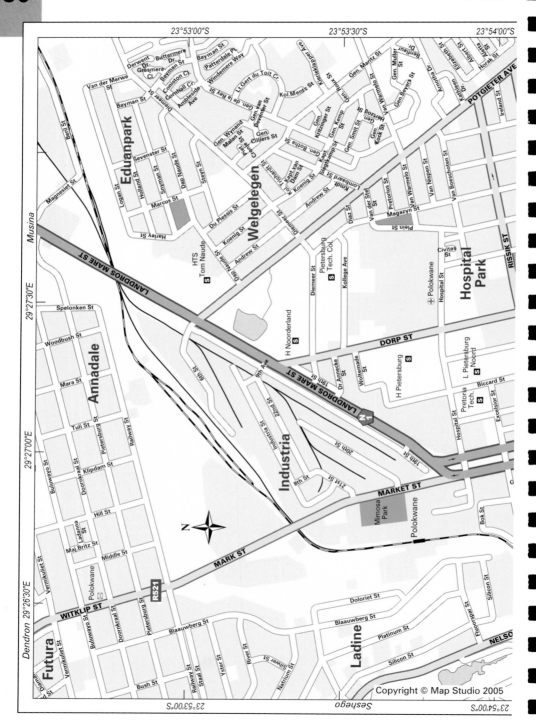

Copyright © Map Studio 2005

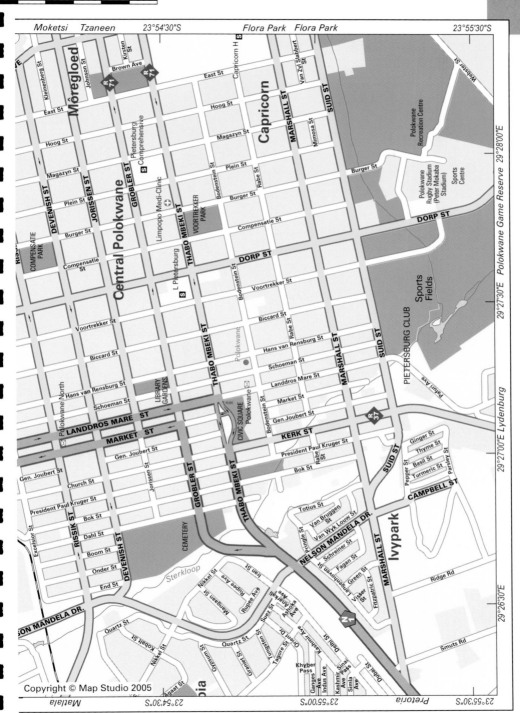

500   1 000m

Kleinenberg St
Johnson St
Kirsten St
Brown Ave
East St
Capricorn H S
Van Zyl Slabbert St
Môregloed

East St
Hoog St
Magazyn St
Plein St
Burger St
Compensatie St

Hoog St
Magazyn St
Devenish St
Jorissen St
Grobler St
Petersburg Comprehensive
Thabo Mbeki St
Voortrekker Park
Plein St
Burger St
Compensatie St
Dorp St

Capricorn
Marshall St
Suid St
Mimosa St

Polokwane Recreation Centre

Polokwane Rugby Stadium (Peter Mokaba Stadium)
Sports Centre

Limpopo Medi-Clinic
L Pietersburg
Bodenstein St
Rabe St
Burger St
Compensatie St

Central Polokwane
Voortrekker St
Biccard St
Bodenstein St
Biccard St
Rabe St
Hans van Rensburg St
Schoeman St
Landdros Mare St
Market St
Gen.Joubert St

Dorp St
Voortrekker St

Sports Fields

Burger St
Dorp St

29°28'00"E
Polokwane Game Reserve
29°27'30"E
29°27'00"E Lydenburg

Polokwane

Polokwane North
Hans van Rensburg St
Schoeman St
Library Gardens
Landdros Mare St
Market St
Civic Square Polokwane
Kerk St
President Paul Kruger St
Bok St

Gen. Joubert St
Church St
President Paul Kruger St
Bok St
Dahl St
Boom St
Onder St
End St

Jorissen St
Grobler St
Thabo Mbeki St
Cemetery
Devenish St
Rissik St
Excelsior St

Pietersburg Club
Bahri Ave

R37
Marshall St
Suid St
Ginger St
Thyme St
Basil St
Turmeric St
Parsley St
Campbell St
Pepper St

Nelson Mandela Dr.
Totius St
Van Bruggen St
Van Wyk Louw St
Schreiner St
Fagan St
Green St
Visser St
Fitzpatric St
Lamgonbahori St
Pringle St
Marshall St

Ivypark

Ridge Rd

Sterkloop

Nikkel St
Rupee Ave
Fran St
Mangaan St
Gyraan St
Quartz St
Kobalt St.
Nikkel St
Granaat St
Suez St
Amethi St
Orient Dr
Tungsten St
Tagore St
Quartz St
Dahi St
Kashmir Ave
Amfolia Ave
Indus Ave
Ganges Ave
Khyber Pass
Kashmir Ave
Sinai Pass
Simla Ave

Smuts Rd

Nelson Mandela Dr.

29°26'30"E

Pretoria

Copyright © Map Studio 2005

**Scale 1 : 22 500**

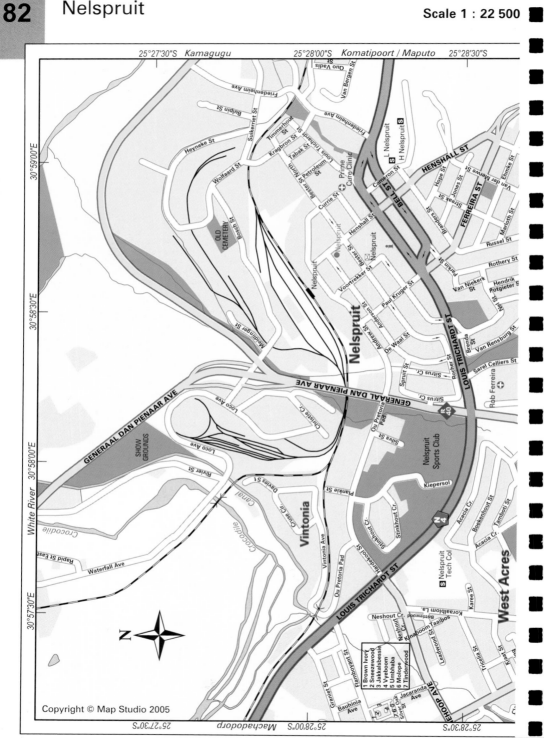

25°27'30"S *Kamagugu*  25°28'00"S *Komatipoort / Maputo*  25°28'30"S

30°59'00"E
30°58'30"E
30°58'00"E
30°57'30"E

*White River*

*Crocodile*

*Canal*

**GENERAAL DAN PIENAAR AVE**

**LOUIS TRICHARDT ST**

**HENSHALL ST**
**FERREIRA ST**

**Nelspruit**

**Vintonia**

**West Acres**

SHOW GROUNDS

OLD CEMETERY

Nelspruit Sports Club

Nelspruit Tech Col

Friedenheim Ave
Buljon St
Suikerriet St
Timmerhout St
Kragbron St
Tabak St
Basen St North
Petroleum St
Louis Trichardt St
Currie St
Henshall St
Cameron St
Bell St
Hope St
Jones St
Strak St
Van der Merwe St
Russel St
Rothery St
Van Niekerk St
Hendrik Potgieter St
Nel St
Van Rensburg St
Sarel Celliers St
Rob Ferreira
Marloth St
Martin St
Bramley St
Paul Kruger St
De Waal St
Rocher St
Brenda
Parkin St
Voortrekker St
Andrew St
Anderson St
Spruit St
Sitrus Cr.
Silva St
Christie Cr.
Loco Ave
River St
Davies St
Plankie St
Stinkhout Cr.
Kiepersol
Cruse Cr.
Vintonia Ave
Hardekool St
Ou Pretoria Pad
Neshout Cr.
Batleywood
Koraalblom La.
Knaboom Taaibos
Acacia Cr.
Boekenhout St
Tambotí St
Karee St
Leadwood
Tricilia St
Kiaat St

Meidinger St
Wolfaard St
Heyneke St
Bosch St

Prime Cure Clinic
Nelspruit
L Nelspruit
H Nelspruit

R40

Z4

Neshout Cr.
Jacaranda Ave
Genriet St
Flamboyant St
Bauhinia Ave
Silver Oak St

1 Brown Ivory
2 Sneezewood
3 Jakkalsbessie
4 Vyeboom
5 Umbhaba
6 Molope
7 Tinderwood

Rapid St East
Waterfall Ave

*Machadodorp*  25°28'00"S  25°28'30"S
25°27'30"S

EHOP AVE

Copyright © Map Studio 2005

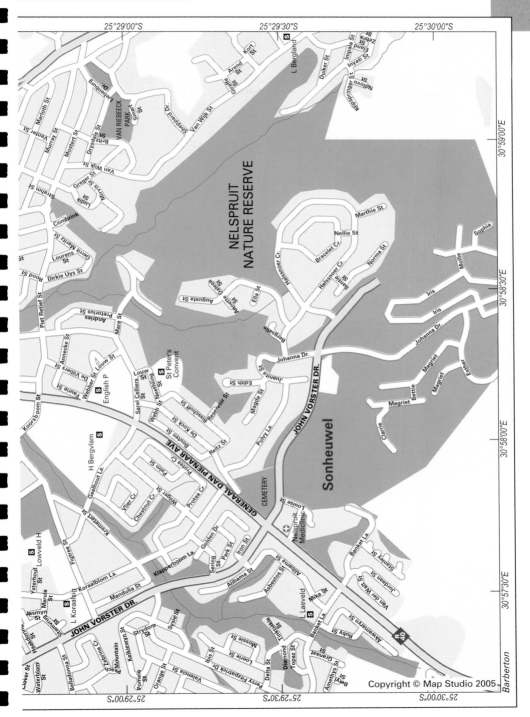

Copyright © Map Studio 2005

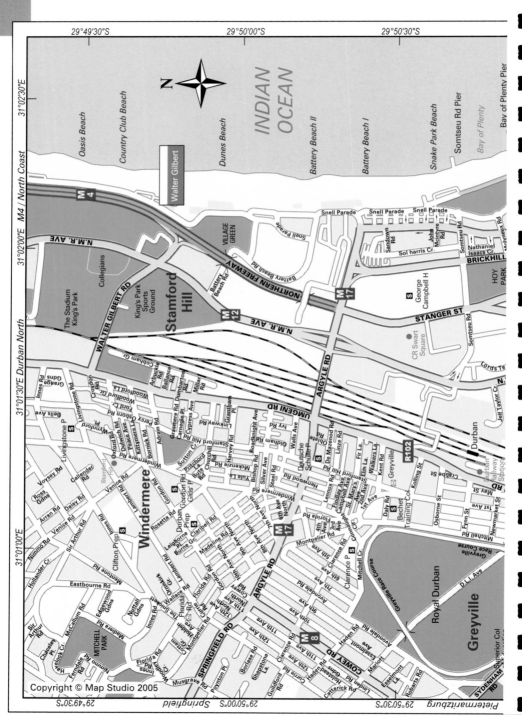

Copyright © Map Studio 2005

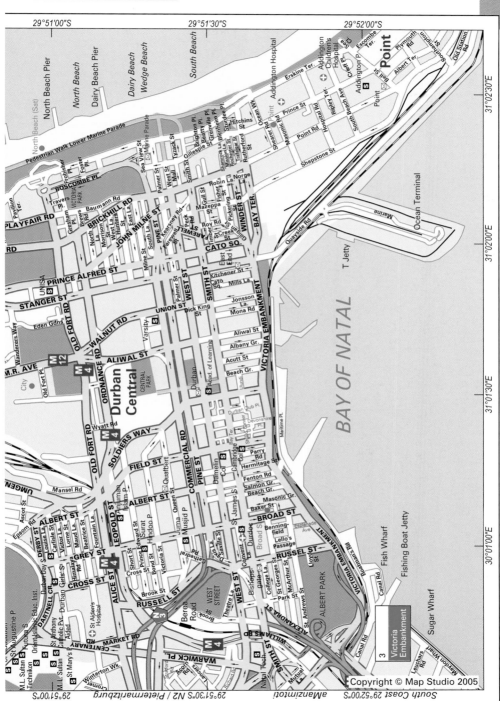

Copyright © Map Studio 2005

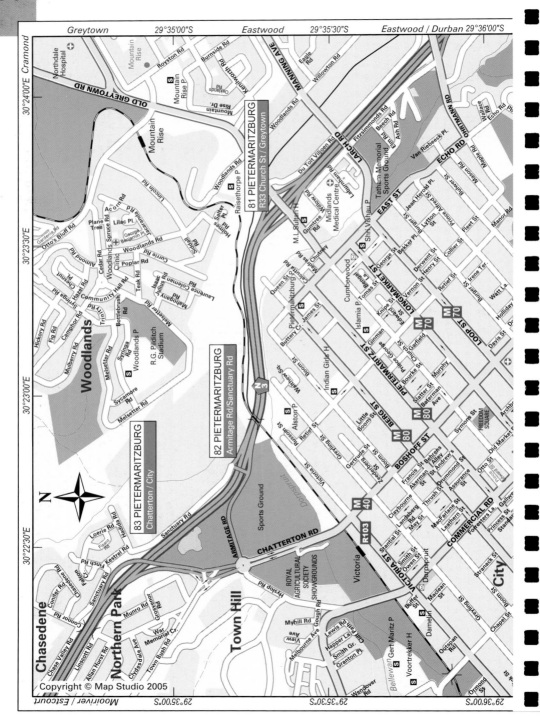

Copyright © Map Studio 2005

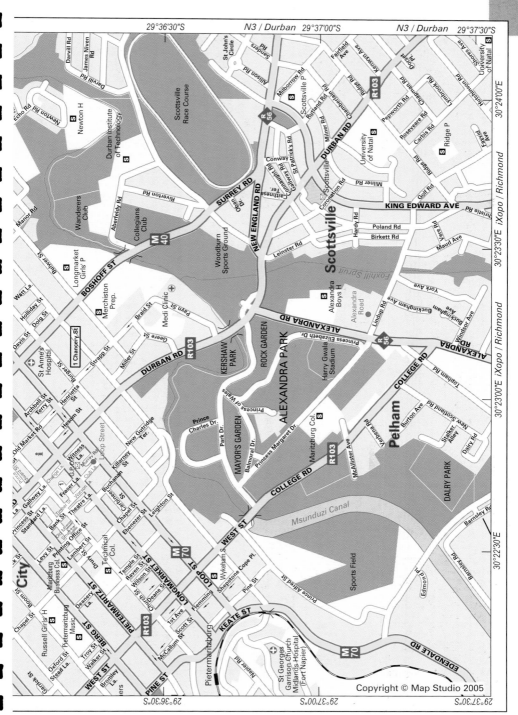

0  500  1 000m

Copyright © Map Studio 2005

# Index to Place Names

**Abbreviations:** E.C. - Eastern Cape  Lim. - Limpopo  N.W. - North West  Gau. - Gauteng
KZN - KwaZulu-Natal  W.C. - Western Cape  N.C. - Northern Cape  Mpum. - Mpumalanga
F.S. - Free State  Zim. - Zimbabwe  Moz. - Mozambique  Swa. - Swaziland
Les. - Lesotho  Bot. - Botswana  Nam. - Namibia

# Index to Place Names

# Index to Place Names

# Index to Place Names

# Index to Place Names

# Index to Place Names

# Index to Place Names

# Amendments ?

As part of our ongoing product improvement programme, we value your input. This information together with your personal details (name and address) can be sent **Post Free** to the following address.

**Freepost CB 11079**
**Attention: The Research Department**
Map Studio
P.O. Box 1144
CAPE TOWN
8000

E-mail Address: research@mapstudio.co.za

## Visit our Website:
www.mapstudio.co.za
**0860 10 50 50**

# Notes :

# Notes :

# Notes :